How to ——— Overcome

DEPRESSION

and other heart-to-heart talks

Printed by:
Mehta Offset Pvt. Ltd.
Mehta House,
A-16, Naraina Industrial Area II,
New Delhi-110 028 (India)

Published by:
Gita Publishing House
Sadhu Vaswani Mission,
10, Sadhu Vaswani Path,
Pune -411 001, (India).
gph@sadhuvaswani.org

Second Edition

ISBN : 978-93-80743-19-6

Printed by:
Mehta Offset Pvt. Ltd.
Mehta House,
A-16, Naraina Industrial Area II,
New Delhi-110 028, (India).
info@mehtaoffset.com

How to ──── Overcome

DEPRESSION

and other heart-to-heart talks

J.P. VASWANI

GITA PUBLISHING HOUSE
PUNE, (INDIA).
www.dadavaswanisbooks.org

Other Books and Booklets by Dada J.P. Vaswani

In English:
10 Commandments of A Successful Marriage
108 Pearls of Practical Wisdom
108 Simple Prayers of A Simple Man
108 Thoughts on Success
114 Thoughts on Love
A Little Book of Life
A Simple And Easy Way To God
A Treasure of Quotes
Around The Camp Fire
Begin The Day With God
Bhagavad Gita in a Nutshell
Burn Anger Before Anger Burns You
Daily Inspiration
Daily Inspiration (Booklet)
Destination Happiness
Dewdrops of Love
Does God Have Favourites?
Ecstasy and Experiences
Formula For Prosperity
Gateways to Heaven
God In Quest of Man
Good Parenting
Gurukul
Gurukul II
I am a Sindhi
In 2012 All Will Be Well
Joy Peace Pills
Kill Fear Before Fear Kills You
Ladder of Abhyasa
Lessons Life Has Taught Me
Life After Death
Management Moment by Moment
Mantras For Peace Of Mind
Many Paths: One Goal
Nearer, My God, To Thee!
New Education Can Make the World New
Peace or Perish
Positive Power of Thanksgiving
Questions Answered
Sadhu Vaswani : His Life And Teachings
Saints For You and Me
Saints With A Difference
Secrets of Health And Happiness
Shake Hand With Life
Short Sketches of Saints Known & Unknown
Sketches of Saints Known & Unknown
Stop Complaining: Start Thanking!
Swallow Irritation Before Irritation Swallows You
Teachers are Sculptors
The Goal Of Life and How To Attain It
The Little Book of Freedom From Stress
The Little Book of Prayer
The Little Book of Service
The Little Book of Success
The Little Book of Wisdom
The Little Book of Yoga
The Magic of Forgiveness
The Perfect Relationship: Guru and Disciple
The Seven Commandments of the Bhagavad Gita
The Terror Within
The Way of Abhyasa (How To Meditate)
Thus Have I Been Taught
Tips For Teenagers
What You Would Like to know About Karma
What You Would Like to know About Hinduism
What To Do When Difficulties Strike

Why Do Good People Suffer?
You Are Not Alone God Is With You!

Story Books:
101 Stories For You And Me
25 Stories For Children and also for Teens
It's All A Matter of Attitude
Snacks For The Soul
More Snacks For The Soul
Break The Habit
The Lord Provides
The Heart of a Mother
The King of Kings
The One Thing Needful
The Patience of Purna
The Power of Good Deeds
The Power of Thought
Trust Me All in All or Not at All
Whom Do You Love the Most
You Can Make A Difference

In Hindi:
Aalwar Santon Ki Mahan Gaathaayen
Atmik Jalpaan
Aapkay Karm, Aapkaa Bhaagy Banaatay Hein
Atmik Poshan
Bhakton Ki Uljhanon Kaa Saral Upaai
Bhale Logon Ke Saath Bura Kyon?
Dainik Prerna
Dar Se Mukti Paayen
Ishwar Tujhe Pranam
Jiski Jholi Mein Hain Pyaar
Krodh Ko Jalayen Swayam Ko Nahin
Laghu Kathayein
Mrutyu Hai Dwar... Phir Kya?
Nava Pushp (Bhajans In Hindi and Sindhi)
Prarthna ki Shakti
Pyar Ka Masiha
Sadhu Vaswani: Unkaa Jeevan Aur Shikshaayen
Safal Vivah Ke Dus Rahasya
Santon Ki Leela
Sri Bhagavad Gita:Gaagar Mein Saagar

In Marathi:
Krodhala Shaanth Kara, Krodhane Ghala
   Ghalnya Purvee (Burn Anger Before Anger
   Burns You)
Jiski Jholi Mein Hain Pyaar
Life After Death
Pilgrim of Love
Sind and the Sindhis
Sufi Sant (Sufi Saints of East and West)
What You Would Like To Know About Karma

Other Publications:

Recipe Books:
90 Vegetarian Sindhi Recipes
Di-li-cious Vegetarian Recipes
Simply Vegetarian

Books on Dada J. P. Vaswani:
A Pilgrim of Love
Dada J.P. Vaswani: His Life and Teachings
Dada J.P. Vaswani's Historic Visit to Sind
Dost Thou Keep Memory
How To Embrace Pain
Living Legend
Moments with a Master

How to Overcome Depression?

God has created a world of
abundance: man, alas! through
his wrong thinking has clogged
the channel through which all this
abundance may flow to him.
All man has to do is to clear the
channel!

How to Overcome Depression?

Shakespeare's *Merchant of Venice* opens with the following words:

"In sooth, I know not why I am so sad..."

Have you ever said this to your friends or even thought this about yourself? If you feel inexplicably sad, or 'low' or unhappy for no reason, you might be showing the early symptoms of depression.

All of us have felt sad or depressed at one time or another in our lives. I read about a brother and sister, a pair of sixteen-year old twins, who were both involved in a plane crash. Fortunately, they escaped alive. But both of them suffered from multiple fractures and were confined to bed for over a year. The girl was delighted with the unexpected break from school. She asked for a TV set to be installed in her room; she asked for a set of CDs featuring all her favourite music; she asked for books; her doting parents who only wanted her to be cheerful and get back on her feet very soon, were happy to meet all her demands. Her mother cooked her favourite dishes for her; her siblings came to her room in turns to entertain her with their non-stop chatter; aunts and uncles spoilt her with gifts and chocolates and flowers and books. When she got back to school a year later, she said to her friends, "Of course it was painful and horrible to put up with those fractures and those dreadful casts and plasters. But I must say, I had a whale of a time!"

As for her brother, he could have asked for and got the same treatment. But he became sullen and gloomy; he hated being in bed; he refused to make the most of his enforced rest like his twin sister. He lost all appetite for food; he refused to take his mind off his condition with reading or music; he became morose and uncommunicative; he lay in semi-darkness, with the curtains closed, and refused to see visitors, even his close relatives and friends.

Feeling depressed is a common reaction in such a situation. People often go into depression after bereavement, an injury, a failure or a loss. Some people can suffer from severe depression when their vanity has been hurt!

For most of us depression is just a transitory mood, a passing phase; but when depression persists, and is accompanied by feelings of intense sadness which prevent us from living normal lives, it is something to worry about. Doctors call this clinical depression – and regard it as a treatable medical condition.

If you read self-help medical guides, you will be quite startled by the common symptoms of clinical depression:

❏ a depressed mood during most of the day, especially in the morning
❏ a sense of fatigue, exhaustion or low energy levels almost everyday
❏ constant feelings of worthlessness or guilt
❏ lack of concentration, inability to take firm decisions
❏ excessive sleeping or lack of sleep
❏ refusal to take an interest in family or community
❏ recurring thoughts of death or suicide
❏ a sense of restlessness
❏ significant weight loss or gain

Experts say that if you have even five of these symptoms, you might be suffering from severe depression.

A friend who read these symptoms on a website said to me that he was startled to realise that he had most of them, almost everyday!

According to the National Institute of Mental Health, USA, it is estimated that, by the year 2020, major depression will be second only to ischemic heart disease in terms of the leading causes of illness in the world. But patients with depression sometimes fail to realise (or accept) that there is a cure to their depressed moods. As a result, they may search endlessly for external causes.

In the US, about 14.8 million adults suffer from major depression, according to the National Institute of Mental Health. The sad thing is that many of these people actually attempt suicide. Unfortunately, most people with clinical depression never seek treatment. Left undiagnosed and untreated, depression can worsen, lasting for years and causing untold suffering, and possibly suicide.

I wish to tell you today of an 'alternative' therapy for depression, which does not involve clinical treatment, medication or psychotherapy.

To begin with, let me tell you about a sister, who served as a school teacher. She was vivacious and full of zest for life. She loved music and dance and she was always the star attraction of every party she attended.

She was a wonderful human being and an extremely popular teacher; she wielded tremendous influence over the students. She was never content to stop her teaching with what was 'in the prescribed syllabus'. She always tried to give her students a little more – a little more wisdom, a little more faith, and lots more encouragement and inspiration. She always began her class with an inspirational thought; she taught the children little prayers that they could say everyday. Little wonder, that the children loved her!

This teacher had a happy family life too. Her daughter was married and well settled in life. The teacher and her husband continued to live a peaceful, happy life in their home. Both of them had great faith in God, and lived happily.

After a few years, as she was approaching retirement, she fell ill. She was detected to have a tumour in the brain, and advised by the doctors to undergo a surgery. She was operated upon successfully, and the tumour turned out to be benign! But, the operation had left her weak and vulnerable. She could not continue with the job she loved. Once she quit her job, she felt lonely and restless sitting alone all day, confined to the four walls of her home.

This vivacious woman, this popular teacher hit the rock bottom of gloom and pessimism. She was depressed. She lost her enthusiasm for living. Lethargy overtook her. She had loved painting and sketching, but she lost all her interest in these creative activities. Her illness had drained her of all energy. It had weakened her physically, emotionally and mentally. As a result, she withdrew herself from her friends. She became even more miserable without the company of her friends, without the job she loved, and without the spirit to live.

Her loving husband persuaded her to consult the doctors. He himself told them what a vivacious and positive person she had been, before the operation. Would she ever be the same again?

The doctors gave her hope and advised her to follow a particular regime in order to bounce back to her original, positive, zestful nature. The first thing the doctors advised was to take up some form of physical activity or exercise. Being in a negative frame of mind, she doubted whether exercise would do her any good. She returned home, rather unsure of herself, but the next morning, her husband persuaded her to go out for a walk. They left home and took a short, leisurely stroll.

As she walked, with slow unsure steps, she felt the fresh morning breeze touch her face gently. She felt her tensions melting away; her mind was relaxed; and suddenly, she remembered the words she had spoken to her students: "You are not alone, God is with you." She realised then, that she had failed to practise what she preached. As she stumbled a little, her husband held her hand gently, and she remembered the words of a prayer she had taught her students: *"Holding my hand, lead me, O Lord. Ever be by my side to protect me, O Beloved!"*

These words gave her strength. A fresh energy seemed to flow through her body. From that day onward, every morning she went out for a walk with her husband; and while walking she reaffirmed the presence of God. This rejuvenated her mind and in this new frame of mind, her heart moved out to her family, her relatives and her friends – all those loved ones whom she had failed to respond to, in her depression.

She began to pray for them, she thanked the Lord profoundly for a loving family, kind relatives and understanding friends. She also thought of the unhappy phase she had passed through; and she prayed for the sick and lonely and those afflicted with sadness.

Gradually, she forgot all about her own physical ailment. She hardly ever thought of herself now. Her mind had shifted imperceptibly to those in need of help and comfort. This attitude gave her immense peace and in that peace she experienced Divine vibrations. She rediscovered herself. She started painting again. Her friends began visiting her. She accepted invitations to attend functions and gatherings, and actually found that she was enjoying herself.

Her doctors requested her to meet and counsel other patients like herself, who had been victims of depression. She gladly agreed and started to share her experiences with others. She said to her new 'pupils', "If you want to live a life of beauty and joy, then you must make prayer an integral part of life."

Pray to God, meditate on His creation, meditate on nature, walk around a beautiful park or up a hillock, travel to a scenic spot or a hill station, admire God's beautiful creation, examine a flower, a petal, a stem, a blade of grass. And marvel at the beauty and perfection of nature. Every flower, every petal, every stem, is a model of perfection and holds the secrets of nature.

Choose any prayer, any verse that appeals to you. Recite it as many times as you can, till it becomes a part of your subconscious mind.

God is protecting us, God is leading us, God is guiding us, God is watching us, God is watching over us; then why should we worry? Why should we fear anything? We must make prayer a habit. Unlike all other habits, it should become integral to our daily living.

As I tell you about this woman, I feel that we should also practise the art of praying and devote atleast one day in a month for prayer, and prayer alone! On that blessed day, we should try to wake up early in the morning, and start the day with a little chat – a soulful, intimate, heart-to-heart talk with God.

It is often difficult to wake up early, but once we have decided to devote the day to God and experience His Divine Power, then it will be easy to pull ourselves out from bed.

Say to Him, "You are not from me afar, You are with me. O God, in Thy strength and Thy wisdom, I shall stand as a hero on the battlefield of life."

The next thing is to thank God, for what He has given us. God who is ever kind and merciful has given us so much. We do not have words in which to adequately express our gratitude to him. After the thanksgiving prayer, read a few pages from a scripture. This helps us in establishing a strong link with God. Choose any scripture, *The Bhagavad Gita, the Sukhmani Sahib, the Japji Sahib, the Upanishads,* the New Testament, *the Torah, the Qur'an* or Gurudev Sadhu Vaswani's *Nuri Bani* or any other scripture that draws you. Pick up those verses which touch your soul and then read the verses carefully, ponder over them and internalise them. After this, think about the jobs. Seek help from God. Seek His blessings, so that you do the job well. Be aware of God's Presence. Things done with the awareness of the Divine Presence are done effortlessly and they are always done well. Be in constant communion with God. While talking on the phone or mobile, while cooking in the kitchen or working on the computer, seek God's Divine Power and blessings. Be aware that you are bonding with the Divine Power and seeking blessings for all that you are doing, and also seeking His benedictions for the people with whom you are working or living.

Spread the sunshine of these blessings all around you. Therefore, offer the loving service of your heart to those in need of comfort and help. Offer solace to a suffering person, do your bit to feed the hungry and clothe the naked and do not forget to feed the animals and birds; for they too, are our younger brothers and sisters in the One family of creation. Make your love universal. With this attitude to life, you are sure to experience miracles. You will feel at peace within, which is akin to *ananda*, pure bliss.

In the rush of life and its mundane activities, we tend to forget the Divine Presence around us. We do not make God real in our life. As a result, we go astray. It is our ignorance that causes us to imagine that God has abandoned us. The fact is that it is we who have abandoned Him, kept Him away from our lives. We have to be firm in our faith. We have to remember Him every moment of our life, we have to bond with God and experience His Presence.

And at night, as we lie down in our beds, we breathe out a prayer to God: "*Ma*! Mother! why should both of us keep awake at night? You never sleep. I surrender myself to You and enter the realm of sleep in the assurance that You are taking care of me throughout the night. Tomorrow morning, I shall wake up fresh and fragrant as a full bloomed flower."

The practice of this way of prayer for just one day in a month, will bring peace and harmony in our life and our life will become beautiful. There will be no room for doom and gloom and pessimism and depression in such a life!

We are not what other people think of us. We are in reality only what we are in the eyes of God!

2

Self-Realisation Overnight!

Our ancient scriptures, describe a lost city that had sunk in the depths of the ocean. Probably it was called the sunken city of the seas. This city, we are told, had many bells, which chimed at the sacred hour of sunset, when the day fades into night; and again, at the break of dawn, when the darkness of the night melts into light. Saints have described the sounds of these chiming bells as sounds of the Infinite – *anahad naad* or the primordial sounds. These sounds are endless and eternal, but can be heard only at the sunset and the sacred hour of *Brahma Mahurat.*

Each one of us should make an effort to hear these chimes. These primordial sounds are eternal. We should search the vast ocean within, where the bells ever chime and sing the melody of harmony.

In the early hours of the dawn the messages of the mystics are heard.

13

Early one beautiful morning, as I sat in silence, I heard a whispering voice say to me, *"Paapi Hoon Gunhaigaar, Rehmaan Mujhe Nihaar, Iss Bhule Ko Ik Baar, Pilah De Apna Pyaar"*. Let me offer the translation of these beautiful words to you: "I am a sinner, I am a culprit. O, Merciful One, give me but a glance of Your forgiveness. Give this wayward one, the nectar of Your love."

Is there anyone among us who can say that he has not sinned? Is there anyone who can frankly say that he has harboured no ill feelings or ill thoughts towards others? We tend to wear many masks, some masks are painted bright and some masks are pure and glowing. But most of us know that they are only masks, the fake camouflage that we put on. We present to the world, an unsullied, pure and beautiful exterior faked to take in others. These masks of falsehood can deceive the world, but not oneself. And in the long run, if we continue to play 'roles' under these fake exteriors, it can cause harm to both our physical and emotional health.

Once, Gurudev Sadhu Vaswani was asked, "Please show us an easy way to realise the Higher Self. We are unable to follow the difficult paths described in the scriptures." Gurudev Sadhu Vaswani replied, "I will show you the easiest way. By morning you would have realised your Higher Self." The devotees surrounding him were happy. Self-realisation in one night! Anyone of them would have thought it was impossible. But here Gurudev was offering us self-realisation on a golden platter.

Gurudev said, "Tonight, you must keep awake; take a sheet of paper, and write on it all the sins that you have committed till now. Tomorrow, early in the morning, you must go and put it up on the notice board outside the Mission Office. Once you have put up the list of all your sins of commission and omission on the notice board of the Mission you will find your Higher Self."

The eager devotees were bewildered. Thoughtful and serious, they retired for the night – perhaps, to keep a vigil, as Gurudev had suggested!

Next morning everyone rushed to the notice board. Alas, there was not a single sheet of paper confessing anyone's sins and the misdeeds. No one was ready to reveal the inner sullied self. Finding the Higher Self could wait!

Human beings have a natural tendency to conceal all their misdeeds. We try to cover them with falsehood, pretense and hypocrisy. The reason for this is of course, our big 'Ego'.

Once, a saint along with his disciples was passing by a graveyard. It was a moonlit night. The very graves shone with the silvery light of the moon. The saint looked at the graveyard, and remarked, "Man is like those graves! See, they appear shining and clean from the outside, but when you dig the graves deeper, you will find nothing but a sordid collection of insects and worms, feeding on dead flesh! In the same way, man may appear very clean from outside, but look deeper into him, you will find venomous snakes of greed, serpents of evil thoughts and wasps of desires. Man's heart is filled with the slush of evil. His mind is full of lust and unhealthy desires!"

Looking at the graveyard, the saint urged his disciples, "Do not carry the dead spirit within. Come out of the graves, and live a life of reality! Do not hide your sins. Do not conceal your crimes and evil doings; do not keep them under wraps. Be natural. Be what you truly are. Not the dead bodies of the graveyard, but the zestful, joyful human beings of the beautiful planet earth!"

We must not be misled by the external gloss. Long ago, in our neighbourhood, a man drove in a big car to 'see' a girl for the ceremony of arranging a marriage. In those days, cars were a high status symbol. Only the very affluent people could afford to have them. The girl was so impressed by the man driving the car to her doorstep, that she told her parents right away that this boy was the right choice for her! The parents, who were experienced in the ways of the world, insisted that they should look into the boy's background, and find out more about him. But their daughter, carried away by the external glitter and glamour, insisted on marrying this boy. After her wedding, the girl discovered to her dismay, that the man she had chosen as her husband, was an ordinary taxi driver. He did not even own the taxi he drove. It belonged to someone else!

The saints therefore caution their disciples not to be swayed by the exterior polish and gloss; but to go in for the intrinsic worth of a man. Appearances are often deceptive. Hence do not go by the face value. It can be as fake as the spurious currency notes which are being circulated by devious elements nowadays.

Do not put up a show for the sake of the ego. Do not be like a fake currency note. You will be rejected not only in the temple of the Lord, but also in the world around you. Be genuine. Follow the truth. Accept your shortcomings, your sins and your faults. Do not hide your weaknesses. Be an open book in the court of the great dispenser of justice. You will be able to cross the bar and withstand the test of time only if you are 'real'.

Do not allow the 'fear' of rejection to come between you and your Beloved. Understand this clearly: you cannot hide your true self from God. He is the Great Forgiver. All that you need is to open your true self out to Him: confess your faults, your weaknesses and your sins. He will surely forgive you and take you up in His loving arms.

A woman of faith and prayer, often asked her son, to bow down before God and seek forgiveness. Her son was an agnostic. He did not believe in God. He would argue, "God is invisible to me. How can I believe in Him?" But the mother, who had a deep devotion and a sense of repentance, pleaded with her agnostic son, to confess his sins and seek pardon.

"Confession of what? Pardon for what?" he would ask, exasperated. "I have done no wrong. I have committed no crime! Throughout the day, I take care not to hurt anyone. I have no reason to seek pardon!"

One day, the grace of God came down upon him. He began to go to a *satsang,* and came in contact with an elevated soul. His mindset changed for the better. He was transformed. He wept tears of repentance. "O Lord!" he cried out. "You have given me this beautiful gift of human birth and I have wasted it in ignorance!"

Not to acknowledge the value of human birth and waste it, is not only gross ignorance; it is a sin. Hence, no one, not even an upright man, can say that he is above sin and sinning. He too needs to confess and seek pardon!

Lord, Thou alone knoweth what is good for us. So many things which appear to be good turn out otherwise and vice-versa. So, let the decision rest with Thee!

3

For Thy Sake

Have you ever asked yourself the question, "What is the difference between an ordinary man and the saints, sages, *dervishes*, men of God?" The difference between an ordinary human being and a man of God is, that the ordinary man goes about doing his work without awareness. But, men of God, whatever they do, right from their daily personal chores to their spiritual disciplines, do so with awareness. A saint or *siddhapurush* is one whose thoughts are pure and who lives constantly in the awareness that God is Omnipresent.

Let us put a question to ourselves – Do we love God? Do we love saints and sages? If the answer is 'Yes', then let our answer to all else be 'No'. The mark of such a man, who loves God and His saints is sacrifice. If my love is without sacrifice, it is selfish. Such a love is a barter, a bargain with God. There is exchange of love and devotion in return for something. It is love which is conditional and 'expectational' if I may use such a word.

There is a true story told to us of a wealthy woman. It was a habit with her to go to the temple and sweep the premises clean everyday. This *kainkarya* (service of devotion) was her offering to the Lord. On the surface she seemed to be an ardent devotee, who inspite of her wealth, did not hesitate to perform menial work. But like all women, she nursed a secret desire. She wanted her daughter to be married to a young, handsome, wealthy, eligible man, preferably someone from America. Such a one came to their town in due course. The woman was very keen to get her daughter engaged to this young handsome man. Everyday as she swept the ground, she prayed to God, "O my Lord, just fulfil this desire of mine. Get my daughter married to this man." A few days later, the woman came to know that the boy was to marry another girl. This unnerved her and shook her faith in God. In fact she became furious and said, "O Lord, You did not answer my prayer. You did not listen to me and from today onwards, I shall have nothing to do with You." This kind of relationship with God is devoid of true love. This relationship is hollow and superficial.

To continue the story, later on, the woman came to know that the boy was already married to a foreigner and he had come to India and got married to a beautiful girl, just to please his parents. It was then that the woman realised her mistake. She repented for her wrong attitude. She thanked God, for saving her daughter from a disastrous marriage. She went to the temple and fell down at the Feet of the Lord.

Pleading for forgiveness, she prayed, "O Lord, I have been foolish and arrogant. Please forgive me. You have protected me from a great tragedy."

True love is selfless. It is prepared to sacrifice. Men of God take birth on this earth, become ascetics and *fakirs*, all for the sake of humanity. They come to mitigate human suffering. They come to heal us and lead us on to the path of Light. They put up with criticism, they go through many worldly trials. Some of them have even become martyrs for our sake. But they have done all this with a smile on their face and with gratitude to God. Unless and until man is willing to sacrifice, he is unable to give love either to God or to mankind.

Once, on one of my visits to Madras, a devotee came over to meet me and said, "Last night I dreamt of you. In the dream, I saw that your mouth was wide open as if you were hungry and waiting to be fed. It was 3 o'clock at night, and such dreams are supposed to be true. And so I got up and prepared 36 varieties of delicacies for you. Now, please eat the food I have brought or else I will feel very hurt."

I explained to her that the sign of true love was sacrifice. True love does not ask for anything. "I wasn't hungry. It was my poor, starving brethren, who are hungry. It is they who have to be fed and not me."

The woman, who seemed very emotional, could not grasp the meaning of what I said to her. She insisted that I partake of the food she had brought. When I asked her what she had seen in my mouth, she could not answer. I told her, "Dear sister, I had opened my mouth wide because the food you have brought is to be fed to my hungry, starving brothers and sisters. My mind constantly dwells on them. It is they who must be fed and served, not me."

The woman remained adamant. She did not wish to distribute the food, which she had so carefully cooked for me, among the poor. She did not love God truly. If she had, she would have said, "All this offering is for You, O Lord. And I know You reside in all, especially the poor and the hungry."

We have all heard of Miss Slade. She was a true disciple of Mahatma Gandhi. She came from a wealthy English family. Her father was an Admiral in the Royal Navy. She was brought up in the lap of luxury and opulence. Yet she left everything, her home, her parents, and her motherland and came to Mahatma Gandhi to live in his *ashram*. When she met Mahatma Gandhi and sought permission to join his *ashram*, Mahatma Gandhi tried his best to dissuade her. He told her that she would not be able to live a life of austerity that his *ashram* demanded of all inmates. Mahatma Gandhi said, "Many women from the royal families have come to live in this *ashram*. But without exception, they have found it difficult to live under the rules, regulations and the strict discipline of our way of life."

But Miss Slade was adamant. She had come to India to live for her ideals, and no discipline could be too tough for her. In fact, the 'call' to go and serve the Mahatma had come to her even when she was a young woman. Having read the biography of the Mahatma by Romain Rolland, the great French writer, she was inspired to leave her family and her home and dedicate her life to the service of the Mahatma. Having read about him and his severe austerity of life, she undertook the most rigorous preparation for her life in India. She had practised austerity and prepared herself in all aspects for the sacrifices that she knew, lay ahead of her. She thought that she needed to put herself through severe training in order to be acceptable at his *ashram*. After having come to that decision, she went through all the chores of spinning, became a vegetarian and a teetotaler, started learning the language, taught herself to squat and sleep on the floor. As for reading, she immediately subscribed to *Young India*. She spent a part of her training programme in Paris, where she read the *Srimad Bhagavad Gita*, and part of the *Rigveda*, both in French. And now, having reached India and presenting herself before Gandhiji, she said to him, "My Gurudev, I am willing to bear any hardship, if I am allowed to be with you."

Miss Slade had lovely golden brown hair. Mahatma Gandhi looking at her beautiful cascading hair said to her, "Can you sacrifice your crowning glory for me? Can you sacrifice your hair?" She left without replying. Mahatma Gandhi and others thought that she found this a hard test and hence she had walked away. But Miss Slade was made of tougher mettle. She went straight to a barber's shop and shaved off her hair. Placing the golden brown hair at the feet of Mahatma Gandhi she said, "Bapuji, this sacrifice is for you."

Miss Slade bore witness to the teachings of Mahatma Gandhi in deeds of daily living. After India received its independence, Mahatma Gandhi's associates demanded high positions in the Government and in the Party. But, Miss Slade whom out of love, Mahatma Gandhi named, 'Mirabehn', did not wish for anything. She wished to continue Mahatma Gandhi's work of village upliftment. She went to a remote corner in the sub-Himalayan region and lived a life of obscurity, offering her service of love to the poor people of the area.

Miss Slade had true love for Mahatma Gandhi and his ideals. She served him faithfully till the end and bore witness to his ideals.

A mothers' love is the only love which is true and unconditional, is it not? There lived a wealthy man with his wife and his only son. The wealthy man passed away leaving behind his large estate and property to his wife and son. The son fell into bad company and squandered away all the wealth that his father had left for him. His wife, for her part, left him taking away all that remained of his money. He became a homeless pauper living on the road. His condition became miserable. Penniless and deprived, he still hankered for his wife. He kept pestering her. Fed up with his evil ways, his wife refused him entry into her house. She said, "If you want to come to me then bring a gift for me. Since you have nothing, you are penniless; all that is left with you is your mother. So the only gift you can bring me is your mother's heart. Go and get it for me."

The crazy man, who was completely out of his senses, went and killed his mother. He plucked out her heart and carried it on a plate to his wife. He was excited at the thought of pleasing her and began to run. On the way, he stumbled and fell into a ditch and the mother's heart cried out, "Son, are you hurt?" This is mothers' love. This is true love.

God too, loves us like the mother in this story. He forgives all our faults and loves us unconditionally.

True love demands sacrifice. What kind of sacrifice should we offer to the Lord? We should sacrifice the ego. "I am nothing, O Lord, You are everything. Nothing belongs to me, everything belongs to You." We must, in fact, make all our actions an offering to God.

A Japanese King wished to build a temple. He made great plans for the temple and was willing to spend millions on it. His subjects also felt that they should pitch in and contribute their might to this lofty venture. The donations were being collected in a huge money-box.

A young devotee of the Lord, who worked as a maid in a household, wished to contribute something to this house of God, but she had no money to put into the box. She was given lodging and boarding in exchange for the work she did, but did not receive any money. Being a true devotee, she longed to contribute something to the making of the temple.

She had long black hair. People simply loved her hair. In fact, a rich young man was so crazy about her long and lovely hair that he had promised to marry her when he returned from his trip abroad. The girl knew in her heart of hearts that her beauty lay in her crowning glory. But, she had nothing else to offer, except her hair. She went to a hairdresser and had her hair cut, so that it could be made into a wig for a fashionable, wealthy woman. The money she received for the hair, she offered as her donation for the temple. While putting the money into the box, a tear rolled down her cheek. She cried, "O my Lord, this is all I can offer You."

The temple was completed after two years. The King invited a saint, a realised soul whose third eye was open, to inaugurate the temple. The saint in his inaugural speech said, "Those present here may think that the temple is built by the King. But, let me tell you, the temple has been built by a humble maid servant." Hearing this, the people were aghast. How could a maid servant build this magnificent temple? Millions had been spent on the temple. The maid servant had no means to pay such a large amount! How was this possible?

"Master, how is it possible?" asked the people. "Go and ask the maid who has made a personal sacrifice for the temple," replied the saint. "Whatever the King has spent is more out of ego than out of charity. But, whatever the maid has put in is out of her sacrifice of the thing that was most valuable to her."

My dear ones, whatever you do, you must do out of selfless love.

Lord Sri Krishna tells Arjuna, "O Arjuna, whatever you eat, whatever you give in charity, whatever austerity you perform, do it as an offering unto Me."

The food you eat – dedicate it to the Lord; the work you do – dedicate it to the Lord. The good or bad that you have to face in the course of your life, think of it as a gift from God. Dedicate all your actions to Him. "All for Your sake! I live for Your sake, I work for Your sake." Such an attitude of offering to the Lord would make your passage through life easier and you will feel light and cheerful.

It is said of a famous cricketer that he had a visually impaired father, who could not see his son's game but always accompanied him to the cricket ground. It was a matter of pride for him to watch his son play the cricket match. After his father passed away, the cricketer's game improved by leaps and bounds, and his scores broke all the records of the game. When asked what the reason for his improved performance, he replied, "Now my father can see me play." If we could adopt this attitude, that our Father in Heaven can see us now, our performance in our daily life would improve greatly.

One way of viewing God is to think of Him as 'Truth' – the Ultimate Truth. God is also love. Hence, the words, 'For Your Sake', mean, building our life on the foundation of love and truth.

A Krishna *bhakta* had intense yearning to go to the Kingdom of Sri Krishna. Every moment of his life he would cry out, "O Krishna, You are mine. I live for Your sake!" It so happened, that one day, he got the chance to enter Krishna's Kingdom. There he witnessed a thought provoking scene. At the entrance to Krishna's Kingdom, stood a *pandit*. He was pleading with the angel who stood guard at the golden gates of Krishna's Kingdom.

"I am a well known *pandit*. I have performed countless *yagnas* and worshipped God through a million rites and rituals. I have studied and memorised and indeed mastered the scriptures. Now, you must allow me to enter the Kingdom of Krishna."

The angel looked at him and smiled. "True, you have performed *yagnas* and worshipped God. But deep within your heart was a desire for recognition by the people. You wanted praise and popularity, worldly fame and glory. You have already received both on the earth."

After a while, as our *bhakta* watched on, a *tapasvi* knocked on the door of Krishna's Kingdom. "Allow me in," he said to the angel guarding the gate.

"What are your credentials? What qualifies you to enter the portals of Heaven?" the angel enquired of him.

"I have practised austerity; I have done penance. I have stood on one leg for months to please Him. I have tied myself upside down on a tree and chanted Sri Krishna's Name."

"We know you have performed unbelievable penance. But within you was the ego that, 'I can do it'. First be free of your ego – come without that heavy baggage and you will surely get an entry into Krishna's Kingdom."

At that juncture, a philanthropist appears and seeks entry into Krishna's Kingdom. "I have built charitable institutions, I have built *dharmshalas* and temples all over. I deserve the Kingdom of Heaven!"

"What you say is true," said the Angel. "All this you did for name and fame. You have done nothing to deserve Krishna's Kingdom of Light."

At this juncture, the poor man who stood aside, waiting for his turn, thought that he had done nothing to deserve an entry into Krishna's Kingdom. As he was about to turn away, the Angel stopped him and said, "Dear one, what have you done on earth, to deserve this privileged entry into the World of Light?"

The poor man said, "I was a poor carpenter. I worked hard to eke out my meagre living. A blind man lived near my house. I fed him, bathed him, and met his needs to the best of my ability. I used to read the scriptures for him. All this I did as a loving offering to Sri Krishna. My one thought was, 'Sri Krishna, for You, the love of You, I do all this'."

"The Gates of Heaven are open for you. Your simple acts of service done with devotion to the Lord are your passport to the Divine Land! You rightly deserve a place in Heaven!"

Small acts of kindness done with true devotion and dedication are more valuable than the gigantic structures built by man in the Name of God. For God needs our true love, He loves the simple and humble way; what Gurudev Sadhu Vaswani called, 'The Little Way'. Follow it and be richly blessed!

We must learn to renounce
everything. When everything is
renounced, God is announced.

4

Learn to Renounce

There was a saint. He was an incarnation of Love Divine. His words were gentle and sweet. He was a picture of compassion. He attracted many devotees, for his discourses were steeped in wisdom and understanding of the human plight.

For ordinary mortals, saints present a riddle. They seem to have a peculiar behaviour. They draw the devotees to themselves and bind them in silken threads of devotion. Sometimes, they pamper the devotees, call them to come close and receive their blessings. Sometimes, they turn their face away and seem to ignore the eager entreaties of the very same devotees. This is a common practice with them; but we need to realise that it has a meaning. In short, it would do us good to remember that whatever a saint does, is done with a purpose.

As we know, both sunshine and shade are essential for a fruit to ripen to perfection. If it receives too much of sunshine, it will wither and die; if it receives too little sunshine, it may not ripen properly. The saints, as Gurus, are responsible for the 'ripening' of our souls. They know what we require, at different stages of our spiritual growth. That is why, saints also follow the same law of nature: from them we obtain both the sunshine of their grace as well as the shade of separation.

This saint had a disciple who was very dear to him. Infact, he would not begin his daily discourse to his *sangat* till this particular disciple arrived. The disciple basked in the warm and radiant sunshine of the saint's loving grace; and then, suddenly, the unexpected came to pass. All of a sudden the saint decided to keep the disciple away from him. The saint would not even look at him or give him a glance of recognition. The disciple was deeply hurt. The saint, who loved him so much, had suddenly turned his back on him. The poor disciple was left yearning for a glance of mercy from him.

As you may imagine, this kind of situation creates uncertainty and insecurity in the mind of the disciple. It makes him feel dejected and left out. This was the experience of the disciple. He felt that he had been abandoned. After all, he had given up all worldly pleasures, broken away from all worldly bonds and made the saint the very centre of his life. And now, the saint had completely ignored him. The disciple felt that he was left out in the cold, completely isolated.

He felt that he had been abandoned by the Guru, whom he loved so much.

Under such conditions the disciple is tempted to give up the spiritual path. Such doubts in the mind are necessary stages in spiritual progress. They help us to face the situation with greater strength. Just as the use of 'dumb bells' or weights in the gymnasium help you to build the muscles of your limbs, so too, these obstacles, doubts and phases of despair help you to fight your own inherent weaknesses and emerge with stronger spiritual muscles.

This disciple also went through the same process. As an eligible young man, he had a good job, several marriage proposals and a great future ahead. He had given up all this to be near his Guru and serve him with dedication and devotion. When the Guru began to ignore him, he was tempted to break that sacred bond and get back to the world of *maya*. He resumed his worldly life. He fell in love with a girl in his office. The girl often shared her problems with him. He had sympathy for her, which in due course turned into love. And then, out of the blue, his conscience began to trouble him. He realised that he had wandered far away from the path of the seeker. He wept tears of repentance. He wrote a letter to his Gurudev, expressing his anguish and agony at the separation from the Master. He pleaded for the Guru's protection and his forgiveness. Life in the company of the Guru was easy, smooth and beautiful and life without the Guru was like walking on thorns. He admitted his mistake in leaving his Master. He concluded the letter with the words, "My Gurudev, please tell me what should I do? How do I come to your door with this guilt in me? Tell me, I have come to seek refuge at Thy Holy Feet."

When the saint received the letter, he was overwhelmed by his disciple's words. The saint immediately replied to his disciple, "Renounce everything and come back to me immediately." By renouncing the world, we step into the sphere of Light. It frees us from the rat-race of running after fame, name and money.

Saints take birth to mitigate human suffering. They try to lead suffering humanity on the path of peace and harmony.

In one of the ancient scriptures we are told the story of a King, who after several years of ruling his empire, renounced it and retreated into the forest. In ancient India, old age was regarded as a stage of life meant for preparation for the Onward Journey. It is the call of the sunset of life when a man must spend the remaining years in prayer. The King we are referring to, retired into the forest to meditate. He lived the life of renunciation and austerity. One day, as he went to a stream nearby to fill water, he saw a deer and its young one on the opposite bank, drinking water. Suddenly they heard the roar of a lion. Frightened, the mother deer tried to jump over the stream to save herself. She was able to jump across the stream, but fell dead on the ground. Her young one, tried to follow its mother, but fell into the water. Seeing this, the King who had now become a holy man, tried to retrieve the young deer and save it. He was able to do this with great effort, and brought the young one into his *kutiya*. For some reason this holy man became very fond of the little deer. It brought life and warmth into his austere life, and he grew very attached to the defenceless creature whom he had saved from the jaws of death. The King who had given up his Kingdom and lived the life of a renunciate, was now trapped in the clutches of attachment. Then, suddenly, the King died. During the last few moments of his life, he was agonised about the future of the young deer. Who would look after the poor animal when he was gone? What would become of the creature when it was left alone to fend for itself in the cruel forest?

According to the scriptures, this holy man was reborn as a deer. But, such was his *karmic* residue, that he was very different from other deers. Whenever he heard vibrating sounds of *mantras* or chants of the Name Divine, he would sit quietly as if trying to listen and assimilate the sound. On the other hand, the pet deer took birth in human form in a Brahmin's house. Right from his childhood he prayed, he meditated on the Lord. He was detached and spent his time in prayers. He had a deep yearning for the Divine.

Fortunate is the man, who is born with this yearning, to achieve self-realisation. Guru Nanak has said, *"Naam Khumari Nanaka, Charhee Rahe Din Raat."* It means, "Indeed, fortunate is the man who is always intoxicated by the Name Divine." This child, the son of a Brahmin, would remain in silence. He would not speak to anyone. People thought that he was dumb and stupid. With the passage of time, he began to spend more and more time in solitude.

The name given to him in the scriptures is Jadabharat. One day, Jadabharat was sitting in meditation under the shade of a tree. The King of that area was passing by, in a palanquin which was carried by three men, one in front and two in the rear. The King looked out from the palanquin and said to Jadabharat, "You are a healthy man. How can you sit idle? In my Kingdom I do not permit anyone to sit idle."

Forthwith the King commanded him to be the fourth bearer of the palanquin. Jadabharat obeyed the King and joined the other three palanquin bearers. However, every now and then, after taking few steps he would jump violently. This annoyed the King, who stopped the palanquin, and began to whip the hapless Jadabharat. He said to Jadabharat, as he whipped him, "Go back to your tree and sit there. You are of no use. Infact, you have caused trouble to me."

At this Jadabharat breaks his silence and says, "O King, I am helpless. For, as we walked on the road, I saw small insects and ants crossing me every now and then. If I stamped them, they would be crushed to death. How could I do that? For, all Creation is One family. The same life that flows through you and me, also flows through these humble insects. How can I stamp on their precious life?"

The King was stunned on hearing these words of wisdom. He realised that Jadabharat was neither dumb nor stupid, but was a man of profound wisdom. The King bowed down before him and touched his feet. Jadabharat achieved *moksha* (liberation from the cycle of birth and death) in that life.

I have narrated this story to make you aware of the fact that even saints have their frailties; saints too, can falter at times. They can also flounder and fall. Once a saint slides down the descent, it is difficult for him to climb and reach the peak. Hence, we should be free from all the attachments that bind us to this world of *maya*, and drag us down from our spiritual pursuits.

How can we learn to renounce the world? So let me show you four ways to achieve this.

1. We must learn to give, give and give without any expectation in return.

    There are two kinds of men in this world, those who always give and those who always receive. It is said that the hand of the giver is always higher than the hand of the receiver. The man who gives is a large hearted man. The large hearted man, who believes in giving, is the man who is not attached to his wealth or money. The large hearted man will keep his needs to the minimum. Whatever he has over and above that, he would give away. If he has four watches, he will keep one for himself and will give away the remaining three to those whose need is greater than his. Gurudev Sadhu Vaswani, always gave us the example of the sun. The sun always gives, it gives its light and warmth and energy to all the Universe. The earth gives its natural treasures to others. The tree gives its fruits for others and does not retain any for itself. The river also flows to quench the thirst of others and not for itself. Learn this important lesson that Mother Nature teaches us. "To give" is one of the fundamental laws of nature.

2. We should not consider ourselves to be 'owners' of anything. None of our possessions is our own. Everything is created by Him.

All things, tangible or intangible belong to God. This realisation will bring detachment. By giving up the ownership of all that you aspire to God, you become free of every bondage.

This world is a stage and in this drama we are merely actors, each here to play our part. We move and act according to the directions from the Above. This attitude brings a sense of detachment. For, we know everything is part of a Divine drama and that the whole drama will eventually come to an end.

A man with this realisation lives for God. All his actions are without any expectation or reward.

Such a man is detached from the world and draws nearer to God.

We become totally free when we surrender ourselves completely to the Lord. Complete surrender gives us freedom from fear and worry, because complete surrender is the path of bliss.

3. We should consider ourselves as travellers or pilgrims upon this earth. This planet earth is not our native home. It is a 'Travellers' Inn' and our stay here is short. It is possible that at the travellers' inn, we may meet people, or make good friends, but after a short stay we must all go our separate ways to our own destinations.

"Ko Kaho Ko Nahi, Preetam Jaan Le Mann Mahi."
"No one is mine, accept the Lord."

We should do our duty and maybe a little more. But we should do it with a sense of detachment. This is the teaching of the great ones. Sadhu Vaswani has said, "This planet earth is a vast desert. In this desert we must live as travellers."

4. The last and most important way is the Socratic injunction: 'Know thyself'. Once we realise the truth of our being, we would be able to overcome our attachments. For, all attachments are either physical, emotional or mental. But, man is neither the physical body nor the mind; the truth is, man enshrines the *Atman*. And *Atman* is *shakti*. Once man realises this that all that he wants and all that he needs is within him, he will not have to wander

outside. He will not run after money, fame and name. Such a man is not 'bound' to the world, but is a free bird in the firmament of the spirit.

My dear fellow devotees, my message to you is this: learn to renounce the world, learn the art of detachment and take a firm step on the path of spirituality. Bind yourself to the truth. Renounce all else.

Let us live one day at a time, in the faith that God is with us in all our struggles and strivings. Let us not hold on to the failures of yesterday, nor manufacture fears for tomorrow.

5

Life is Short, Let Us Make it Sweet....

One day, as I was walking through the solitude of the woods, I recalled the sacred words spoken by my Beloved Gurudev Sadhu Vaswani, "Life is brief. Our stay upon this earth is but for a few days."

People tend to forget that life is ephemeral. Sometimes, I think they do not realise that they themselves are mortal! They speak and act as if they will live forever; they want to possess things – possess things permanently! They cling to their possessions as if they own them for eternity. People are so obsessed with their belongings, their houses, their cars and all their wealth that they do not want to part with them at any cost. I see many families around, bitterly divided over property matters. They fight with bitterness over their share of land, houses and other possessions. An advocate once told me that several pieces of prime real estate in Pune, worth hundreds of crores of rupees,

44

are lying vacant and disused because the brothers of the family are involved in bitter court battles lasting for years!

I knew of two brothers, one of whom lived in the US, while the other lived in India. The brothers had a dispute over the family property. The younger brother decided to go to the US to settle the dispute and to claim his legitimate share. But alas, on the very day he reached the US, he breathed his last. This man perhaps carried within his heart, the weight of years of bitterness and anxiety. The discord between the two brothers had hurt both of them. The conflict served no purpose. In fact, one of them left this earth disgruntled and unhappy.

The Jewish scriptures tell us that property is a sacred trust given by God; it must be used to fulfil God's purposes. No person has absolute or exclusive control over his or her possessions. The concept that people have only custodial care of the earth, as opposed to ownership, is illustrated by this Hebrew story:

Two men were fighting over a piece of land. Each claimed ownership and bolstered his claim with apparent proof. To resolve their differences, they agreed to put their case before the *rabbi*. The *rabbi* listened but could come to no decision because both seemed to be right. Finally he said, "Since I cannot decide to whom this land belongs, let us ask the land." He put his ear to the ground and, after a moment, straightened up. "Gentlemen, the land says it belongs to neither of you but that you belong to it."

Leo Tolstoy the great Russian writer has said, "When two brothers fight over the property and want to divide it, God above, laughs, for all land is His, and our life is too short to be wasted in bitterness and hatred."

People often put a question to me, "What is the purpose of our life if we are supposed to live without our wealth and possessions?" Others want to know, "Why should we not fight for what legitimately belongs to us? That would be only fair and just."

True, you must claim what you think is your own, as long as it does not break homes, bifurcate families and bring disharmony and turbulence in life. For, the aim of life is to cultivate the soul and to experience peace and bliss. One important element of living is to love unconditionally. For love without sacrifice has no meaning.

Most people live life on the surface. They live a superficial life, unaware of the goal or the meaning of their life. This life, as I said earlier, is given to us not to possess and own, but to love and give and share whatever we have with those less fortunate than we are. Life is too short; why should we waste our precious time in conflicts, quarrels and court cases? Instead, we should patch up all our differences, and live in harmony with one another, for time is running out for all of us. Death can claim us at anytime; and then, it maybe too late.

Once there lived a King. One day, a man came to visit his court and presented to him a large and exquisitely carved hand-fan. The King opened the fan and was astonished to see a beautiful painting displayed on it. The King was very pleased. He used the fan for a long time. When it was old and began to fall to pieces, he gave it to the court jester with the words, "Keep this fan with you. When you meet someone more stupid than you, then you may give it to him." The King had meant to mock the jester.

Many years rolled by. The King was quite old now. One day, he fell ill. The doctors declared that he would not live long. At that time, the court jester sought permission to see the King. He knew that the King was very close to the end of his earthly journey. The jester requested the doctors, "The King has been very kind and merciful. He has looked after me very well and I am greatly obliged to him. I would like to have a last glimpse of him."

They allowed him to visit the King. Bowing down to the King he humbly asked, "O King, how are you? How is your health?" The King replied with great effort, "I am ailing. The *vaids* have given up all hope. My end is near and now I have to embark on a long journey."

The jester asked the King, "How long is that journey?"

The King replied, "It is a long, long journey."

"How do you know that it is a long journey?"

"I have heard it said, and indeed, I have read from books, that it is a very long journey indeed."

"You know that it is a very long journey. Have you prepared for it?"

The King was quite startled. He replied, "No! I have made no preparations for this journey."

Upon hearing this reply, the court jester took out the hand-fan from his pocket and presented it to the King. He said, "O King! You had given me this fan to be passed on to the one who was even more foolish than I. Today, I give this fan to you because although you knew that a long onward journey awaited you, you did not bother to prepare for it. O King! Can there be greater ignorance than this?"

My dear friends, let me share a secret with you. It is only at the very end of the earthly journey when we look back upon our life, do we realise the time that we have wasted in futile pursuits. But as the saying goes, 'It is never too late'. You can begin from now; and prepare for the long, onward, forward journey, that we all have to undertake sooner or later.

The best way to prepare for the onward journey is to make the best use of the 'now'. Discharge all your duties with love and devotion, continue with your daily routine but along with all these activities, remember the Name Divine. Believe me, this will help you to be more efficient in your work, and you will feel better in every respect. Your emotions will be more positive and your speech will become sweeter.

There are many paths to achieve the goal of life—i.e. liberation or *mukti*. The easiest path is *bhakti marg*.

This path is of devotion, this path, perhaps is of surrender; this path leads to the destination of *mukti*. In moments of agony, in times of stress, each one feels the suffocating pressure of worldly life. It is then that we cry out, "Let me be out of this. Let me live and not merely exist." Perhaps, the easiest and the best way to free oneself from this suffocation would be to follow the path of *bhakti*.

There comes a stage in everyone's life which becomes the turning point for transformation. Saint Mira was a queen of Chittorgarh and she lived a royal life amidst luxuries. But the luxuries hurt her. She did not want to live in delusion. A time comes in her life when she pulls herself out of that suffocation. She chooses the path of *bhakti*. She is fully transformed. She becomes the spiritual seeker, the singing saint, intoxicated by the nectar of Divine Love.

Mira was a spiritual genius. In one of her songs, she sings, "*Mera Mann Lago Hari Jeso, Ab Na Rahungi Atki.*" It means, "My heart belongs to the One God (*Hari*) and nothing can hold me back." Mira moves through the villages, through the deserts and forests, singing the glories of her *Shyam Sunder*, affirming that she will be free from the cycle of birth and death. Nothing will pull her back into it.

As I said earlier, life can be really suffocating. I receive letters from young men and women, letters that express anguish and anxiety. My question is, "Why suffer and struggle in this desert of life? Why not fill it with the nectar of *bhakti*? As long as we are attached to the world and run a rat race to fulfil our desires, we are bound to feel empty, hollow and suffocated.

In the Srimad Bhagavad Gita, Sri Krishna tells Arjuna, "O Arjuna, I shall share a secret with you – *Renouncing all writ duties come unto Me! For, I shall free you from all the bondages of suffering.*"

The Lord promises us redemption if we totally surrender ourselves to Him. Total self-surrender brings peace and bliss.

Each one of us is in quest of peace. Even the richest man is in search of peace and harmony. Peace cannot be bought with money or wealth. It has to be cultivated within.

Two thousand years ago, a holy man said, "Nothing have I when I wake up in the morning, nothing have I when I go to sleep at night. And yet, I am the richest man on earth, because, I am at peace with myself."

The message that he gives us is this: be in tune with your inner self and be at peace with all around, because you are, in essence, a peaceful soul. We must retain this peace by following the path of devotion and self-surrender.

When will the day dawn when my mind, oblivious of all else, will be completely immersed in Thee? When will tears of longing and love flow from my eyes, as I repeat the Name of the Beloved:- "Krishna! Krishna! Radha! Radha!"?

6

The Transformation of a Tawaif

"**O** friend, my every breath belongs to Him, my Beloved!"

The beautiful song of St. Mira reverberates in the air, re-echoes in our hearts, bringing with it the timeless message of love and longing for the Lord!

Fortunate was Mira, blessed was she, for she had surrendered her life to her Beloved Sri Krishna! Mira, in all her songs, yearns for one thing above all else— her Beloved, her Divine Love! She cries, "I need nothing, nothing at all. I need but a glimpse of my dear Beloved." Her yearning recalls the cry of the *sufi* soul, desiring nothing but the union with the Beloved— The Supreme Being.

I need nothing, Mira cries. Alas, how many of us can say the same with her! We need so many things. We need money; we need luxuries; we need cars and houses; we need better and more expensive clothes and jewels. Man's wants are many and keep multiplying!

But saints like Mira, have only one need – the need to see the luminous face of the One who for want of a better word, we call the Supreme Being. This longing, this awareness of the pain of separation is one of the traits of true devotion; and it is a rare quality. Only very few people, who have reached the heights of spiritual growth, are blessed with it; this longing for the Beloved, manifests itself as an unbearable affliction: "Ah! This separation is an unbearable pain!"

This overwhelming emotion arises only when we are the receptors of grace from above. This shower of grace can come anytime. It can fall on anyone. The moment the grace is showered, the inner urge is awakened. That becomes the turning point in one's life. Sadhu Vaswani often spoke to us about the Law of Transformation. One twist, one unexpected turn in life, and you are reborn as a new person.

There is a story told to us of a woman of ill repute. One day she receives the grace of God. She is born anew; her life is touched by grace and she is transformed into a new being. Abandoning her ignoble profession, she moves to the holy city of Varanasi. There on the banks of the holy River Ganga, she makes a boat her home. She begins her *sadhana* of incantation of the *Rama mantra*. Soon the word spreads, that there is a holy woman who lives in a boat on the banks of the river. Hoards of people visit her, venerate her, touch her feet. She tells them, "Do not touch my feet. Touch the feet of Lord Rama! I am nothing. He is everything." But still, people continue to touch her feet out of deep devotion. She writes on her boat in bold letters, "I am not a *sadhvi*. I am not a saint. I am a sinner! If you want to touch anyone's feet, touch the Lotus Feet of Sri Rama."

How did this transformation come about in the life of this woman of immoral character? The change was brought in by a young man of high spiritual power.

This young man was studying in a college. At the end of the year, when the exams were over, he had a long vacation. He went to his Guru, and asked him, how he could use this long vacation for his spiritual gain; for he was keen to make some progress towards his goal in life. The Guru offered him a simple suggestion for self growth. He told him to go to a particular village. There by the side of the river, he would find a cremation ground. "Go there," the Guru said, "and spend your time in meditation. You will be blessed with an unforgettable experience."

The young man accepted the Guru's advice. He went to the village, and by the river, he found a cremation ground, just as the Guru had said. He put up a small thatched shelter there and began to live in it. He cooked his simple food there, ate, prayed and spent most of his time in meditation – even while dead bodies were being cremated nearby. The funeral pyres, as you can imagine, were not a happy or encouraging sight; but the experience of living in constant sight of death, gave the young man a sense of *vairagya*. "Well, it is good to get used to this sight," he said to himself, "for one day, sooner or later, you too shall be there, cremated and gone, leaving behind nothing more than a handful of ashes!"

The young man lived a life of this kind of discipline for 39 days. On the 39th day, he grew tired of living on the cremation ground, watching dead bodies being burnt. "My friends must have enjoyed their vacations. They must have had a great time. Why am I rotting here?" he mused. "The Guru had said, that I would have many unforgettable experiences, but so far, I have had no such experience, except a feeling of despondency." The young man felt that he should leave the village and return to his home town now; there were two more days of the vacation left; he could relax and enjoy himself for those two days at least, after his grueling stint in the village.

And so, he decided to quit. He dismantled his straw hut, and bid goodbye to the cremation ground and decided to return to his home town. It was pitch dark when he passed through the village. As he crossed a lane, he heard a sweet melodious voice singing, "The journey is long, the time is fleeting, so hurry up, if you want to reach the goal!"

The young man was enthralled. The sweet voice had captivated him. He enquired from the people around, about the singer, "O she is a *tawaif* (professional entertainer)", they explained. "She has a sweet enchanting voice." Struck by those words, "The journey

is long......run, run...if you wish to reach the goal",
the young man realised that he had made a mistake by
giving up his *sadhana*, at this point in time, when just
two more days were left. He immediately went back
to the cremation ground by the river.

On the 41st day, the young man had the unforgettable
experience that the Guru had promised. He felt a
beautiful sense of calm and serenity. He experienced
a state of stillness. It was a mystical experience, the
like of which he had never had before. He felt deeply
grateful to the *tawaif*, whose song had awakened and
rekindled in him the desire to go back to his 'discipline'
and carry out his Guru's instructions. The young man
became an ascetic, and in his saffron clothes, he went
to meet the *tawaif*. The sentinel at the door pushed
him away, saying that this place was not for *sadhus* and
saints. Hearing the commotion at her door, the *tawaif*
herself came out. Seeing the young man in his ochre
robes, she said, "O man of God, you have come to
the wrong door. Perhaps, someone has deliberately
deceived you, and misguided you!"

The young ascetic, replied, "I have come to the
right place. I have come here to meet you." After much
persuasion, he was able to gain entry into the house.
The first thing he did, was to kneel and bow down
to the *tawaif*. "You are my mother!" he exclaimed with
tears of gratitude in his eyes. "You have taught me
a great lesson. Thanks to the moving words of your
beautiful song, I have reached my goal! But for your

song, I don't know how long I would have wandered in the wilderness of the dark."

The *tawaif* was surprised; how could her seductive song have influenced a *sadhu*, she wanted to know. How she could have brought him on to the right path?

The young *sadhu* then narrated to her, how his weak will and impatience had compelled him to abandon the path shown by his Guru. Her song, "The journey is long, the time is fleeting, hurry, run, run fast to reach the destination…" had enlightened him and he had resumed the life of discipline prescribed by his Guru. And the reward for his discipline had come to him, even as the Guru had promised; he was now on the pilgrim path to the Homeland of the Soul.

The *tawaif*, for her part, was profoundly moved by the youth's experience. She had sung the song to entertain her customers for years together; but she had never understood its real meaning. Now, enlightened and awakened, she too decided to turn over a new leaf. She gave up her immoral profession, and resolved to go to Varanasi, to seek her salvation.

On the banks of the sacred Ganga, she became spiritually empowered by the chanting of *Sri Rama Naam*. She entered into the state of super-consciousness. She lived life on a higher plane, forgetting everything else. She could even predict her death. A day before her final farewell, she folded her hands before her devotees and said to them, "I take your leave today, for tomorrow I shall embark on my final journey!'

A few words can bring about the transformation that we all seek. Once the transformation happens, then even those who are running after worldly wealth will sing, as did Mira – "I need Thee and Thee alone!"

Krishna! I am Thine, completely Thine! Take me in Thy shelter and shield me from the magic charms of this maya-ridden world!

Beware of Maya!

If there is one thing our saints and sages constantly warn us about, it is against falling a prey to *maya* – worldly illusion. *Maya*, can vanquish the best amongst us ordinary mortals. It is only the company of the saints and the *Satguru*, which can assure us of protection against the lures of *maya*.

Several legends and oral traditions have grown around the composition of Sant Kabir's *dohas*, as indeed around the *bhajans* and *slokas* of the great saints. I would like to share with you one such story.

Once, Sant Kabir was earnestly entreated to visit the home of one of his devotees. The man, who was quite wealthy, was very particular that the saint should bless his new home by residing there for a few days at least. Sant Kabir was shown around the huge, palatial residence. The devotee said to him, *"Guruji,* consider this house as your own. Please choose whichever room you like, and I will get it ready for you to stay."

Sant Kabir smiled his mystical smile. "My needs are few, and your house is vast," he observed. "I only need a small room for my brief stay here. I suggest you give me one that is not required for other uses, for I want you to know that I shall stay here with you on one condition – under no circumstances must you ask me to vacate the room, until I choose to leave of my own accord."

The wealthy devotee was delighted to hear this. "Why would I ask you to vacate your room?" he beamed. "It is my ardent wish that you should make this house your permanent residence! You can stay here just as long as you like, and I assure you, you will not be disturbed on any account."

Sant Kabir looked around, and chose the smallest room in the house for his stay. The devotee protested that the room was too tiny, and offered the grand, large rooms that were available; but Sant Kabir gently declined the offer, and moved his simple personal belongings into the room. "I hope you remember my condition," he reminded the disciple. "I have deliberately chosen this small room so that you may not be put to inconvenience on my account; but you must not ask me to vacate this room, once I begin my stay here."

"*Mahatma!* Am I such a low creature in your eyes that you should think me capable of such irreverence?" he protested. "This house is yours. No one will ask you to move out of this room as long as you grace it with your presence. In fact, my dearest wish is that you should be here forever and forever, and we may drink the nectar of your wisdom everyday!"

As Sant Kabir settled into his new accommodation, he happened to glance outside the window, and saw *Maya*, the Goddess of Illusion, standing in the garden. She was surrounded by treasure chests full of silver and gold and precious gems. She smiled at Sant Kabir, as if to say, "I will have you vacate this room sooner than you think." Sant Kabir too, smiled at her, and went about his work.

Later that day, the devotee looked out from his window, and saw *Maya* at her feast – eating from her golden plate, drinking water from a golden cup. Seeing the prosperous condition of the Goddess, the wealthy devotee was smitten by greed. In his heart of hearts he thought that if this beautiful Goddess, the embodiment of wealth and gold came to live with him, he would become even more wealthy. So he rushed out into the garden fell on his knees before her and implored, "O dearest *Devi*, please come to stay in my house for a few days. Choose any room you like. The whole place is yours."

The Goddess went around the house, and deliberately chose the room occupied by Sant Kabir. The wealthy devotee was caught in a dilemma. Putting on a false smile he said, "How can you live in this small room? The whole house is yours! I beg you to choose a finer room that would be more suitable to a grand Goddess like you." But *Maya* was adamant. "If I have to stay in your house, I would like to stay in this room and not in any other. If for some reason you are unable to offer me the room I have chosen, then I will go and stay with my other followers."

The wealthy devotee was so overcome by greed that he decided then and there that he would not let the Goddess leave his house. He was so envious at the very idea of her choosing to go to one of his neighbours! Under no circumstances could that be tolerated! As for his Guru, well, he could always be tempted or cajoled to occupy some other room.

He went inside the room and said to Sant Kabir that he was constrained to ask him to vacate the room for a special guest. Sant Kabir, of course, had been expecting this to happen. Nevertheless, he solemnly reminded the devotee of his earlier promise. But the wealthy devotee was so obsessed with the greed of gold that he said to Sant Kabir, *'Mahatma,* I am sorry about breaking my promise. But, it is imperative that you vacate this room now. You can choose any other room in the house."

Maya, standing at the door of the room, was smiling and staring at Kabir as if to say, "See I have triumphed over you. People need me more than they need you." Sant Kabir in his own humble way smiled back, as if to say, "Sure enough. I'm moving out to live with another devotee of mine. If you can throw me out from there, then I can accept that you have won and I have lost."

Sant Kabir packed his bags and made his way to the humble cottage of a poor devotee. Seeing Sant Kabir at his doorstep, the poor man was beside himself with joy. He said to Sant Kabir, "My house is small, but my heart is large. You can live here as long as you wish."

Sant Kabir replied, "You have very kindly invited me to stay with you. But are you sure that you will not ask me to vacate the place for any reason? Because if that is the case, I can go and stay elsewhere." The poor devotee replied with tears in his eyes, "This house may not be large or grand; but it is all I have and I place it at your disposal. The entire house is yours. If you wish, my family and I can move out of the house and arrange to live in a *dharamsala*, so that you may continue your life of prayer and chanting of the Name Divine, undisturbed by our presence."

Sant Kabir assured him that that would not be necessary, and occupied a corner of the house, where he set out his belongings. Following his footsteps, *Maya* arrived at the same house. She threw her golden plates and golden glasses, all around. The poor devotee watched her dramatics, unperturbed, but did not utter a word.

Maya cast her alluring glance on him and said to him, "I wish to stay in your house for a few days. But, I want for myself that corner which is now occupied by Sant Kabir."

The devotee replied, "That corner does not belong to me. It belongs to Sant Kabir. How can I offer you something that does not belong to me?" Disappointed, *Maya* said to him, "If that be the case, then I will go and live elsewhere." The devotee remained nonchalant. He said, "You may stay wherever you want. But the corner is occupied by my *SatGuru*, Sant Kabir, and it cannot be vacated for you under any circumstances." Sant Kabir threw an intense glance at Goddess *Maya* as if to say, "Look, I have won." He began to sing a *doha*: "*Nake Kati Kane Kati, Kat Kut Ke Daari, Santan Ki Berani, Tirlokan Ki Pyari.*"

Perhaps the message which Sant Kabir wished to give us is this – that the wealth not amassed by fair and just means, is not worth possessing. To accumulate gold and silver you may lose your Soul. You may have to compromise on your self esteem and your true worth. You may have to suppress the truth and reality in order to accumulate gold and silver. In other words, amassing wealth may involve wrong practices and even sinful methods.

I was recently told of a young man who was sent abroad for higher studies. His family was good and there was nothing lacking in his upbringing. His father wanted to give him the best of education. He was sent abroad. The father bore all the expenses, taking care of his needs and comforts. On his return the young man found his father ill and confined to bed. The young man forgot all that his father had done for him. He was unwilling to shoulder the responsibility of caring for an old ailing father. He secretly enquired of the doctor, whether mercy killing would be permitted. He was not only shirking his duty but, was also harbouring the evil thought of coming into all the vast property his father had struggled hard to build.

Can there be anything more dishonourable than this?

The greed for wealth is really the greed for *maya*, for nothing is more ephemeral and illusory than the possession of wealth. Rightly did Sri Ramakrishna warn us against the lures of *kanchan* and *kamini* – love of gold and love of women, the twin evils of *kama* (lust) and *lobha* (greed). Believe me, greed and lust can really make you blind and deaf to all else. Do not fall into such a situation. Do not become a slave, a worshipper of money. Let not money rule your mind. Instead let the mind rule money. Whether you are rich or poor, what matters is the wealth of your inner self, the peace and the serenity of your inner self which is more valuable than all the wealth of this world.

It was Guru Arjan Dev who said, "God, who is Omnipresent, who is our Father, is often neglected by us. We care more about the things which are mere outward shows, and not for those true values which matter to our inner self." He ends this observation with a question: "Why do you love the things which imprison you? Why don't you bond with the Eternal?"

Today, man finds himself in a miserable condition. A saint who saw the truth of the human condition sang, "Living in the house of wet sand, you pamper your senses." For all worldly ambitions carry the seeds of pain and suffering with them. At the end of the day, when the house of sand collapses, the seeds of pain and misery will sprout and you will find there is no escape for you.

It is in the lower nature of man to live a life of greed, lust, anger, attachment and descent. Man wastes his time in harbouring negative thoughts. These sinful and evil thoughts bring agitation, irritation and anguish. Man does not realise that every breath of his life is precious, and each breath, each moment, should be used positively. When man realises this truth, he cries out, "O Lord, let me take refuge at Your Lotus Feet, I need nothing else. All the glamour, the wealth, money, gold and power are but an illusion. Let me be away from this illusion and walk the way of truth."

Once we asked Sadhu Vaswani, "What is this world? What is this life?" He replied, "This world is a death-trap. The wheel of death moves continuously. It can cast its sharp arrow at anyone. We have taken birth many times, we have lived many lives and we have passed through the door of death many times." That being the cycle of death and birth, we should realise that there is no time to be wasted in the pursuit of illusions.

Iran has produced many saints and *dervishes*. One of them was the *dervish* Yaya Khan. His message to his disciples was, "Remember that death is knocking on your door. So be awake and welcome it."

One day Yaya Khan's brother wrote to him a letter, in which he expressed three wishes of his. Two of the wishes had already been fulfilled. But the third one remained unfulfilled. His first wish was to spend his last days at a holy place. This wish had been granted to him. His second wish was that he should have a maid servant to take care of him. By the grace of God he had a loyal and faithful servant, who took good care of him. His third wish, which was as yet unfulfilled was, that he should have the *darshan* of his saintly brother.

In reply to this letter, Yaya Khan wrote to him, "It is true that a place becomes holy when a saint lives there. If you can become pure then the ambience of that place becomes pure. Please remember there is only One Master and we are all His servants. Can one servant employ another servant? You desire to have a servant to take care of your health. But you yourself are a servant of the Master. From that perception you had no right to ask God for a servant. You desire to see me simply because I am your brother. Before meeting me, first go and purify your heart. You should purify your heart, purify it to the extent where there are no desires left and all the world is your friend. If you wish to make your life beautiful, then I humbly suggest that you lose yourself in Divine Love. You belong to Him and Him alone."

The Holy Ones have but one message for us: "Be in the world, but belong to Him, who is your Lord."

To conclude, do not waste your time and energies in negative activities. Do not succumb to the lures of *maya*. Focus yourself on the positive goal of life. Remember, our time here upon earth is short, and the onward journey is long. Hence, make a beginning right now.

If you would grow in the power of endurance, learn to be patient. The highest endurance is patience!

8

Faith and Patience Go Hand in Hand

Two things are essential for every aspirant who wishes to make progress on the spiritual path. The first is to cultivate patience; and the second is to have absolute faith. In this, as in so many other things, nature is our teacher. If only we observe Mother Nature, if only we would appreciate her splendid panorama in all its wondrous magic, we would perceive that nature does not hurry, it is never in haste, and everything happens in its due course. Look at the sun, it religiously rises in the morning and sets in the evening. This has gone on for centuries, and it will continue to do so for centuries to come. The sun keeps shining, giving its light to the earth and sustaining all the creatures on it. The sun never changes its course; it never fails in its task of affording light and warmth to us.

Likewise, the trees stand firm in sunshine and rain. The trees do not complain, in fact they bless us by providing us with shade, fuel, wood and fruit. A tree is invaluable to man. And yet we pay no attention to its presence or indeed acknowledge the many benefits we receive from it.

Very often I have heard people complain that they work very hard, but do not receive adequate reward or recognition for their efforts. Once I met a man who was perhaps going through the same experience. He said that whenever he felt his efforts were not appreciated, he would go to an area where men were laying new roads. Here, he would watch the labourers breaking stones, tirelessly. These men keep hammering the stones in order to break them into rubble. The labourers keep on at this back-breaking work ceaselessly. They continue with the drudgery of breaking stones day in and day out for a pittance, which is often barely enough to feed their large families. Their patience and untiring, uncomplaining effort, is something that spiritual seekers would do well to emulate.

Let me tell you about one of the most powerful and persuasive orators of ancient Greece. Demosthenes was a professional speech writer or logographer. He gave his own first political speech in 354 BC, and it was a disaster! The words literally choked in his throat, and they would not come out! Utterly discouraged, he sought the help of a professional actor who helped him to train his voice and taught him the art of speech delivery. But it was an arduous task! Let me give you the words of his biographer, Plutarch:

Hereupon he built himself a place to study in under ground (which was still remaining in our time), and hither he would come constantly everyday to form his action and to exercise his voice; and here he would continue, oftentimes without intermission, two or three months together, shaving one half of his head, so that for shame he might not go abroad, though he desired it ever so much.

Demosthenes was not deterred by failure. Instead, he resolved that he would empower himself and strengthen his will and determination in order to be a good communicator. He remained firm in his resolve. With great patience and hard work he was able to awaken the *shakti* within, and went on to become one of the most popular and respected speakers of his time. His powerful speeches remained in the minds of the people for a long time. All the achievers in the world have had these two qualities namely – patience and unshakable faith.

Many a time we lose patience and give vent to anger. This way we harm ourselves.

Once there was a King. He had a pet eagle. The King was very fond of the bird. He would often talk to the eagle making it a part of his daily conversations. He carried the bird wherever he went. He loved the bird dearly. One day, the King went out hunting. As always, his eagle was with him. In the hustle and bustle of the hunt, the King was separated from the rest of his retinue. He was lost in the dark depths of the jungle, with only his eagle for company.

After hours of futile wandering, the King felt very thirsty. He looked around for signs of water. Far away he noticed a weak drip of water. The King walked up to the place and placed a cup under the tiny drip of water. It took quite a while for the cup to be filled. He was about to take the cup to his lips and drink the water, when his beloved eagle pounced on it and spilled all the water. The King was agitated. He looked at the bird angrily, as he began the slow and painstaking process of filling the cup yet again under the dripping water. Again the bird pounced on it and spilled all the water. This happened three times. Furious, the King took out his sword and slashed the bird into two. The bird which he had fed and nourished with his own hands, was killed by those very hands!

A little while later when his anger subsided, he thought, "What have I done? I have killed my beloved bird with my own hands." It was then that the King noticed a dead body lying near the source of the dripping water. The water was contaminated. The bird was trying to save his life, but he had not realised it. He had lost all patience, and in a fit of blind rage he had killed his beloved bird. The King felt guilty and miserable.

Very often in life we lose patience. Once, a socialite went to see a play in a theatre. The play was long and it got over late. When the woman returned home, she discovered to her dismay that the diamond necklace she was wearing was missing. Next morning, she searched high and low for it, but it was nowhere to be found. After that futile exercise, she thought that she had probably dropped it at the theatre the previous night. She immediately called up the theatre manager and told him about the missing diamond necklace. The theatre manager politely told her that the theatre was yet to be swept and that it had not been cleaned after the previous evening's performance. If she would wait for sometime he would look for it and get back to her. The theatre manager did find the diamond necklace but the angry, impatient woman had disconnected the phone even before he could complete his assurance. In her impatience she forgot to leave her name, telephone number and address. The theatre manager was helpless. He tried his best to search for the woman but all to no avail. The woman lost her precious diamond necklace – because of her anger and impatience.

Patience is a great virtue. It helps us to grow on the spiritual path. This path, as we all know, is difficult. It has many obstacles. Without patience we would never be able to tread this path. Even for those of us who do not aspire to spiritual progress, patience is vital in our daily dealings. With patience one can solve one's own problems and help others as well. Patience brings rhythm and harmony into our chaotic lives. And as I said earlier, Mother Nature too follows the law of rhythm.

There are many people in this world, who epitomise patience. There was a nurse in a hospital who looked after her patients very sincerely and devotedly. In her ward was a seriously ill patient. His condition was critical and the doctors had ordered that he should be kept off all food and water, and put on drips. The nurse would attend to him everyday, and considering him as an image of God, she would serve him dutifully. With her tender care and loving concern, the patient improved and the doctors gave him permission to eat food. The nurse brought him the prescribed diet – a boiled egg.

The man who had starved for so many days went into fury at the sight of one egg. Losing all his balance, he picked up the egg and threw it at the nurse. The nurse was a picture of patience. She coolly wiped her face and smiled at the man. Once again, she brought him an egg to eat, but the patient lost his cool and threw the egg on her face. When this was repeated for the third time, the nurse went up to the patient and tenderly said, "You are my brother. Why do you throw these tantrums? The doctors are limiting your food for your own benefit. All these days you were not given any food and now that you have an egg to eat, would you just throw it away?"

Hearing these words the patient softened and tears rolled down his cheeks. He asked, "Am I your brother? Tell me, where did you learn so much patience?" The nurse replied, "I have learnt patience from my

Guru." The patient had come from overseas. He was so impressed by the nurse and her sweet nature that he expressed his desire to meet the Guru and become his disciple.

In this world of haste and waste, stress and tension, trials and tribulations, patience assumes great worth. Patience is necessary to avoid dissipating our energies. Patience makes life smooth and stress-free.

Gautama the Buddha had a worthy disciple. This disciple decided to leave the *ashram* one day, in order to seek self-realisation. He resolved that unless and until he achieved this goal, he would not return to the *ashram*. He felt it was essential to be on his own, so that he could meditate on his inner self and perhaps, reach the goal. Living with other disciples in the *ashram* appeared to him as an obstacle on the spiritual path. Hence, he sought solitude in order to work his way to *nirvana*.

Being alone without the company of those on the spiritual path, can sometimes have a negative effect. The intense loneliness of the mind can give vent to suppressed desires. This is exactly what happened to this *bikshu*. All kinds of evil thoughts troubled his mind. He lost his sanguine and pious nature. After years of fruitless effort, he returned to the *ashram* without accomplishing his task.

The inmates of the *ashram* asked him, "Have you found the truth?" The *bikshu* replied cynically, "There is no truth. I wish to give up this pursuit of knowledge and go and live in the world as an ordinary person." The others tried to convince him that he should not leave the path midway, but pursue his spiritual journey with renewed devotion and patience. They further impressed upon him the need to meet the Master. They took him to Gautama the Buddha.

Gautama Buddha said to him, "O son, why do you want to give up so easily? Why have you lost your patience?" The *bikshu* was unable to answer. Buddha held him in his powerful gaze of illumination, for a minute. Then he said to him, "O dear one, do not lose patience so easily. There was a time when you saved five hundred lives. Why do you despair now?"

Hearing this, the *bikshu* weeps. He repents his decision to leave the *ashram*. The words of Gautama the Buddha restore his faith in life. The *bikshus* of the *ashram* are surprised. They humbly ask the Master, "How did he save five hundred lives?"

Buddha smiles and says to them, "He is known to you only for a few years. But I have known him from many lives. In one of his previous births he was the servant of a well-to-do merchant. Once, the merchant loaded his caravan and went to trade in a neighbouring country. The merchant's caravan had five hundred people and nearly as many camels. The caravan had to cross a desert. The journey through the desert was to take 28 days. The caravan had a guide who showed the way through the desert. As the desert was very hot and inhospitable the caravan moved during the night and rested during the day, pitching their tents to shield themselves from the blistering desert sun. The caravan had carried food and water only for 28 days. On the 27th day the ration of the food and water was over, but the merchant thought to himself that they would surely reach their destination within 24 hours.

As fate or fortune would have it, it so happened that on the night of the 28th day, the guide was sleepy and tired. He misguided the caravan so that it travelled in the wrong direction. Next morning, when the sun rose the merchant realised that they had reached the same place where they had pitched their tents the previous day. Exhausted and thirsty, the merchant was at a loss, as to how he would provide food and water to his people, who were under his care, and his moral responsibility. However, he had great faith in God. He prayed to God fervently, and sought His help. Suddenly he noticed at a distance, a spot of green, underneath a giant stone. "There should be some water over there," he mused. The merchant's men started digging around the stone but could not find water. The merchant pressed his ear to the stone and he could hear the rustle of running water. He called his servant and asked him to break the stone. As the servant broke the stone, water gushed out from the seams. The merchant's men were happy. The sight of water infused a new life in them. They quenched their thirst with the cool waters of the stone and also used it for bathing.

Buddha said, "In that life, I was that merchant and this *bikshu* was my servant, who broke the stone and saved the lives of five hundred men."

Let us not give up our effort on the spiritual path. Let us not lose courage, but cultivate the virtue of patience, and face the challenges of life with equanimity and fortitude. Let us continue with our *sadhana* and with our prayers.

Prayer is a powerful energy. Prayer is a request which is always acknowledged. Prayer can work miracles in our life. Therefore, let us make prayer an inseparable part of our life.

Prayer has the power to transform. St. Augustine was born of a noble family. Unfortunately, he got into bad company and began to live a sinful life. He actually began to live with a concubine. His parents lived in a different city. When they come to know of his sinful ways, they felt miserable. His mother wept and prayed to the Lord to save her son and redeem him from his sinful ways. "O Lord, grant him a new life", she kept praying – not for a day, a week or a month but for years together. She was a woman of faith and believed that her prayers would be answered. After very many years there was a remarkable transformation in Augustine's life and he became a saint of God.

So let me urge you, do not lose patience easily, be strong willed. Cultivate the strength within. Do not be irritated by minor irrelevant incidents, do not waste your energies on futile discussions and debates.

Let there be no war of words that drain you of all energy. Keep your mind under control and focus your thoughts on things that ought to be.

Without patience it is difficult to make spiritual progress. Therefore, cultivate the twin virtues of patience and faith.

The ego is a thief; the ego is our most dangerous enemy; it is the force that separates the Soul from God. It is the impenetrable wall which hides us from the Light with dark shadows of 'I', 'Me' and 'Mine' falling on us, obstructing our vision.

9

The Caged Bird

We live in a cruel world. The other day, as I was strolling down the beach, I noticed a shop with beautiful birds imprisoned in cages. The caged birds were for sale!

I think a bird in a cage is one of the saddest and cruellist sights in the world. Imagine trapping a marvellous winged creature whose element is the vast wide open skies, clipping his wings and imprisoning him in a cage for your pleasure! What kind of pleasure is that!

'Birds' are big business in some countries, especially exotic, multicoloured, birds with brilliant plumage. People fall in love with these exotic feathered beauties—but they do not set them free! Instead, they pay exorbitant amounts to take them home in a cage and watch them sing and chirp in their expensive 'prisons'. And they reassert that they love these pets ever so much! What kind of love is that which keeps the object of love imprisoned?

Have you ever thought about the agony of being imprisoned in a cage? The helpless birds flap their wings, striking against the iron bars. Birds which are supposed to be free and flying in the sky, are caught, tortured to be caged behind bars. Seeing the plight of these beautiful birds, a man who was accompanying me on my walk, was moved to pity. He was a kind and a compassionate man. He purchased all the birds and released them in the Hanging Gardens of Mumbai. How happily we saw them fly away!

With folded hands, I plead with all of you to be kind towards animals and birds. Animals and birds are your younger siblings in the one family of Creation.

Germany is known for perpetrating torture in the concentration camps during the World War II. It is a known fact, that Jews were tortured and put to death in gas chambers by the thousands. The treatment meted out to the prisoners of war was inhuman and unjust.

You, as awakened human beings should condemn such atrocities. You should raise your voice of Truth, and stand by it. No matter what the punishment, be true to your 'human' nature and uphold human values of peace, non-violence and freedom.

If we try to understand the perfect scheme of creation, and the oneness of all life, we would be ashamed of the cruel acts perpetrated on animals. Think deeper. You will realise that in this oneness, killing an animal or eating it is nothing short of cannibalism! If we kill these beautiful creatures, who have intelligence and emotions, aren't we worse than barbarians who slaughter and inflict pain at the slightest provocation? For animals and birds do not even provoke us. They are our friends and benefactors; and we repay them by killing them mercilessly. I hope sense will dawn on the children of the New Age, and they would value birds and animals as precious gifts from God, and treasure them as incarnations of His beauty.

Seeing the caged birds in the 'Pets' store, I thought to myself, that we humans are no better than the caged birds. We are born free, like the birds. Freedom is our birthright. We should be flying in the open skies, and touching the splendour of rainbows. But we are caged by desires, by the 'bars' of 'ego'. We are prisoners of our own selves. We have to break free; we have to find our wings and fly away in order to seek liberation. Instead we have locked ourselves into a tiny cage of the self called, 'EGO'.

Our whole life is spent in hectic activity. The poor spend all their lives running around for two meals a day. As for the rich, they too are running an exhausting race to earn more and amass more! We are bonded slaves of our own 'little' self.

Have we pondered over the true treasure, the intangible wealth which is with us? We are all peaceful souls. We all have the rich treasure of *'shakti'* and *'shanti'*. We have not explored these. We do not even attempt to find these treasures within and enjoy them, experiencing the joy and happiness of freedom.

We have heard of the story of Yaksh and Yudhishtira. In this fable, Yaksh asks Yudhishtira many questions. One of the questions asked is, "What is the most strange thing on this earth?" Yudhistira's reply, "The most strange thing is that man bids farewell to his dear and near ones; he sees people depart from this world. He watches the funeral pyres being lit; he sees the dead body burn to ashes at the cremation ground, but does not realise that one day he too would be like that or a dead body on the funeral pyre."

This body is given to us for a limited period. It is given to us as a vehicle to reach our final goal of salvation. Guru Nanak has said, "So many are hungry, so many are ill. So many suffer." But God has been kind to us, He has showered his grace on us, He has given us a healthy physique and higher intelligence. He indeed takes care of us! The third thing He has provided us is the love for *satsang*. We should let that love grow. We should not be lured by worldly temptations. We should learn to say 'No' to all that which takes us away from the joy of *satsang*. For, *satsang* will empower us with true *shakti*; it will enrich us with true treasure of peace and happiness. In our weaker moments, we should not succumb to despair. We may consult astrologers and numerologists, but we do not need to feel low because of their unfavourable predictions. Our destiny does not lie in our stars or in our numbers. It lies in our attitude, our effort and God's grace. Besides, we must constantly reaffirm to ourselves, that there is the power house of *shakti* within us. Gurudev Sadhu Vaswani used to say to us, "Look within. Know the *shakti* that is within you."

It is strange that the *'shakti'* which helps us to exist, is unable to see its own source. We are obsessed with the visible, but deny the invisible only because of its source which is hidden from itself. We are unable to see the splendour within. This is probably because we cling to the base nature and psyche of the human mind. Greed, jealousy, envy and competition, muddy the waters of the spring within. And in that harsh dryness, we forget the gentle, sweet and rhythmic flow of the waters of the spirit.

Do not allow yourself to be wrung dry by the greed of the world! Allow the flowing waters of the spirit, to spring fountains of joy from within. Be aware. Be awakened. Keep chanting the Name Divine. Make this a habit. Let chanting the Name Divine be an automatic, natural process, which fills the mind, whenever it is empty. Keep the mind occupied in the most natural way. Just as you walk or sit or do any routine work almost 'automatically', so too, in the same way, chant the Name Divine. After constant repetition, the Name Divine will become a part of your life and nature.

Let the Name Divine synchronise with your breath. The chanting will become as natural as your own breath. Once that happens, your whole life will change. And you will no longer be a bird in the cage. You will be like a bird flying high on the firmament of the spirit.

If you move in the company of holy ones, something of their holiness will penetrate your life and fill you with holy vibrations and aspirations. That is the value of daily satsang!

Are We Prepared to Pay the Price?

Saints are a storehouse of *shakti*. Saints are a source of positive, Divine Energy. They receive and radiate this energy through their special connectivity with the Lord. Saints are so bonded with God that His Divine *Shakti* flows through them. This is why we often see them perform what we regard as 'miracles'. Their healing, restorative, superhuman power is directly drawn from God.

Sri Ramakrishna Paramahansa was a saint par excellence. He would go into *samadhi* at any time of the day. Sometimes, while giving a discourse or talking to his devotees, he would go into a trance. His soul would leave the physical body and meet the Eternal. Sri Ramakrishna Paramahansa was known for this. He would be so absorbed in the Absolute, that he would forget his physical existence. His disciple Swami Vivekananda was fascinated by Sri Ramakrishna's ability to enter into the state of super-consciousness. As a young man studying in college, he asked Sri Ramakrishna Paramahansa to teach him to have the same experience. Sri Ramakrishna asked the young man, who was then known as Narendra, to lie down on the ground, and actually put his foot on Narendra's chest. By the very touch of Sri Ramakrishna's foot, Narendra lost his consciousness and experienced the state of super-consciousness.

As I narrate this incident to you, I am reminded of a young man who had requested Gurudev Sadhu Vaswani, for the same grace. In 1944, Gurudev Sadhu Vaswani visited Kolkata. He also visited Jamshedpur, which is an industrial township built by Tata Iron and Steel Company. Jamshedpur is famous as the steel city, for the very first steel plant in India was built there by Jamshedji Tata.

During our stay in Jamshedpur a young Parsi man visited us. He had heard Sadhu Vaswani's lecture on the Gita and was deeply impressed by it. He followed Sadhu Vaswani wherever he went, seeking to be his disciple. He said to Sadhu Vaswani, "Bless me, so that I may achieve the goal of my birth. I have practised austerities, I have led a life of discipline, and I have longed to walk the way of a seeker. The one thing that I lacked was the grace of a Guru and now, I have found you. Kindly shower your grace on me."

He begged Sadhu Vaswani to teach him to reach the state of super-consciousness. For, he was eager to experience that bliss. He added, recalling the anecdote that I have just narrated to you, that Sadhu Vaswani should make it possible for him to experience the same bliss or *ananda* that Vivekananda experienced through the grace of Sri Ramakrishna!

In answer to his request, Sadhu Vaswani merely smiled. Time and again, this young man would follow Sadhu Vaswani and plead with him to make him his disciple as Sri Ramakrishna had made Swami Vivekananda his dear one. One day, this young Parsi man became so insistent, even obstinate with his request, that he wanted to be transported to the state of super-consciousness then and there. He declared that he would not move from there, unless and until he had experienced *samadhi*.

Sadhu Vaswani smiled and asked him, "What price are you willing to pay for it?"

The young man replied, "I am ready to pay any price. You name it and I will pay it. But, I want to experience the state of super-consciousness here and now. I am not prepared to wait any longer."

Sadhu Vaswani said to him, "Alright, young man, I appreciate your determination. I want you to go and shave your head right now." Gurudev added, "After shaving your head, go and attend to your office as usual. But, don't cover your head with a hat. And in the evening, after office hours, come back to me and I shall give you what you have asked for."

The young man left at that very moment and we never saw him again! Probably, he thought, how could he go to the office with a shaven head? His colleagues would laugh and make fun of him.

Many of us are like that young man. We ask for the grace of the Guru, but we are not willing to pay the appropriate price for it. We wander, we search for bliss, but are not prepared to pay the price. Sri Ramakrishna Paramahansa had thousands of devotees but he chose to bless only one of them Narendra because Narendra was ready for that experience. Swami Vivekananda was a pure soul, who had earned rich treasures of the spirit, during his previous births. All that he needed was the touch of the saint. That touch removed the veils of illusion in a moment and made him see the Absolute Reality. Saints choose those souls which are ready to embark on the spiritual journey. They may bless and be kind to all their devotees. They may even shower their choice benedictions on them. But it is only the ready soul, the alert and awakened soul who gets the opportunity to be led by the Master on the tough spiritual incline that one must climb to attain liberation.

The main problem with man today is that he is full of desires. His life is full of the negative emotions of lust, anger, greed, attachment, ego, envy and jealousy. It is a common observation that when the lady of the house pours milk into the vessel, she first washes it and cleans it thoroughly. Otherwise, the milk will curdle, on contact with the impurities in the vessel.

In a similar way, we have to cleanse our interiors. We have to purify our inner self. We have to make it clean, so that we can find our true reflection in it. If we have spiritual aspirations, then the first step is to make ourselves gentle, clean and pure.

When Sri Rama went to Rishi Vashishta to receive his benedictions, he was told, "God can be realised within a moment." True, God can be realised within a moment, provided the heart is pure and the mind is clean. His abiding grace is all around us; but we have to be ready to receive the grace. The trouble is, the grace is always there but we are not ready to receive it.

Gurudev Sadhu Vaswani often told us that God is very near to us. In fact, God is within us. The question we often put to him was, "Why is it that we cannot see God?" Sadhu Vaswani would reply, "Look at the mirror on the wall. It is greased. We are unable to see our own reflection clearly. You will be able to see your clear reflection, only when the mirror is clean and shining. In the same way we will not be able to witness the Reality unless the heart is purified. Once the interior is clean, pure and shining, then a glance, a touch, a word from the Master is enough to experience that Supreme Bliss."

Of course, the grace has to come from above, for such a miracle to happen. For this we have to prepare ourselves. That is why, time and again, I plead with you, to begin the preparation for the long journey ahead.

It is good that many of us go to the *satsang*, as that is also a part of the preparation for the onward journey. However, I am afraid that many of us who go to *satsang*, do it as a diversion. We do not bond genuinely with our fellow *satsangis*, we do not read and ponder over the scriptures. I often wonder: how many of the devotees of Sadhu Vaswani have actually read his sacred scripture, the *Nuri Granth*? How many of them remember the sacred words? And, how many of them imbibe the teachings of the great Master? Often our physical bodies are in the *satsang* but our minds wander far away.

Who is a true *satsangi*? Not the one who attends the *satsang*, but one who absorbs the pure vibrations of the *satsang*, listens to every word carefully, goes home and ponders over the teachings and puts them into practise. At times, hundreds of devotees come to *satsang*, but I cannot help thinking that only a handful among them have true spiritual intentions. But, it does not matter. Some of these devotees will surely reap the benefits of the pure and sacred environment, while the others will make a beginning in the right direction.

There was a devotee who had regularly attended *satsang* for 30 years. His son, a young man, often wondered why his father attended the *satsang* everyday. What could he possibly gain out of it? So, one day, he decided to accompany his father and attend the *satsang*. He listened to the discourse, about the Creator, who is our Father, our Protector and our Guide. He heard the speaker say, "All Creation is one family. We all are His children and therefore, we should help one another." The words touched him deeply, and he carried these words in his heart.

Next day, when he went to open his shop, a cow came along and put her mouth in the sack full of wheat. This young man, having heard the discourse in the *satsang*, was awakened. He realised clearly that all creation is one family and that it was his duty to feed the cow. So he gently patted the cow, as she nibbled the wheat.

When his father saw this, he rudely admonished him; "Can't you see the cow is ruining our grains? Don't just stand there, drive it away!"

The son replied, "How much can the cow eat? 1 Kilo, 2 Kilos or 3 Kilos at most? That will not make us poorer. For God has given us enough."

The father was astonished. He asked his son, "Where did you learn this lesson?" The son replied, "Dear father, I attended the *satsang* yesterday and this was the lesson I learnt there." Hearing this, the father was unhappy. He told his son, "Whatever you hear in the *satsang* is only for that moment. Once you leave the *satsang* hall, you, forget all about it and learn to live a practical life."

That is why I said, a true *satsangi* is the one who carries the message of the *satsang* with him, imbibes it and puts into practise. We all should be true *satsangis*.

Satsang is the most potent means of energising and elevating your subconscious mind, through powerful spiritual vibrations that emanate from the Guru. This is reinforced by the faith and aspirations of one's fellow aspirants who congregate there. Such good association can only do us good, by aiding our moral and spiritual growth.

11

The Rain, it Raineth Everyday

I have always loved stormy weather. The rain and the thunder and lightning capture my heart and seem to cast a magical spell on me. I love to watch the rolling waves of the ocean under the pouring sky. Stormy weather creates its own mystical beauty which is fascinating and astonishing. I love to watch the crackling sky and the brilliant lightning shimmer through space and vanish in the vast emptiness. In fact, I love to go to Mumbai during the monsoon, when the rains are at their peak and nature is at the height of her power, vitality and vibrancy. It is difficult to tell you about this powerful, awesome beauty, for it has a quality of divinity about it, which cannot be described but can only be experienced.

Let me attempt to share one such experience with you. Once I was travelling to Mumbai during the rainy season. All along the way it was beautiful. The flowers had blossomed with the touch of rain and the rocks were covered with myriad colours of green. In between the rocks and the niches, the rain water cascaded and tumbled, forming small streams and miniature waterfalls all along the road. Everything around us looked green, alive, vibrant, fresh and rejuvenated. The rain had washed away all the thick layers of dust, which summer had inflicted on the trees and rocks. I am sure you too, must have noticed how the rains have this magical quality of cleansing and transforming the very landscape of India: it seems as if the rain gives a fresh coat of green all around, and somehow makes everything look new, fresh and absolutely enchanting! Mother nature's ways are indeed mysterious and captivating!

If you have ever taken the old highway from Pune to Mumbai during the monsoon, you would have seen hundreds of people actually getting drenched, indeed, soaking wet in the rain, as they take in the freshness and the life-giving quality of the pure rain water. Seeing the splendour of the monsoon, I said to myself, "This rain, our life-giving south-west monsoon, falls only during four months of the year. But, there is the rain of grace, which falls continuously on us, all our lives, sweeping away the accumulated dust and dirt of a dead past. Alas, why do we not get drenched in this shower of abiding grace?"

We in India, are very particular about our morning bath; for many devout souls, it is almost a ritual. We take a shower every morning; we bathe and clean our bodies with soap and water. We clean our physical bodies, but, we rarely cleanse our inner self.

Gurudev Sadhu Vaswani often used to tell us that there are three kinds of rain. The first one is the pure waters of the *satsang*. These Divine waters flow through *sankirtan*, through the sacred words of saints and from the scriptures. They flow from the positive circle of the continuous incantation of prayers and *mantras*. These waters of the *satsang* cleanse your interior, and give you an integration of mind, heart and soul. These waters purify you even as the holy waters of the Ganga cleanse you from within. The waters of the *satsang* are indeed a source of great purification.

The very word *satsang*, means fellowship of truth and truth as we know, is a hard taskmaster. Truth is ever vigilant and like a sentinel stands brandishing its iron weapon, preventing any unauthorised entry into its domain. For inside the domain of truth, there is only truth, there is One Name, One Shyam, One Rama and One Love. Once you enter this domain you cannot come out. *Satsang* of the true type permits you to glimpse this realm; it enriches, empowers and beautifies the inner self.

The second type of rain is the experience of the interior world. You can contact this source of grace through meditation and silent communion with the Divine.

The third type of rain is experienced through selfless service. People go to a great extent to 'decorate' or beautify their homes; they spend millions on buying signature paintings. They spend vast amounts on exotic carpets and rugs, exclusive objects of display, and luxury emulsions to adorn their walls.

Millions are spent on the exteriors of the houses, designed by architects whose fees alone could provide homes to a dozen homeless people! This kind of extravagance, in a country where 30 million people are said to live below the poverty line, is conspicuous as an indication of our new culture of 'consumption'. There are seriously afflicted people in this country who have no money for their medical treatment, desperate parents who are unable to get their daughters married and in these times of recession, there are many who have lost jobs or are on the verge of losing their jobs and their very livelihood.

How can we, in all conscience, indulge in such personal extravagance amidst all the poverty and misery of our fellow human beings?

We all need to have the experience of selfless service. This is like a shower of blessing and joy that invigorates our very spirits. We should spare at least a part of our expenses to be spent in the service of the poor. The waters of selfless service have a magical effect on the body, mind and spirit. It washes away the 'I' of ego. It washes away the cobwebs of the mind and the lower emotions of the heart. Selfless service washes our inner instrument or *antahkarana*, and leaves us with a lasting feeling of joy that no personal extravagance can ever match! Selfless service should be undertaken with a feeling of devotion. It is an offering to God!

A word of caution to my workaholic friends. It is true that all work is worship of God; and we should put maximum effort into whatever we wish to achieve. But, work should not be killing! It should not drain your spirit or kill you with the slow poison of stress, anxiety and fear. Your work should not cripple you. My dear ones, do not become workaholics, create time for your own self. For, ultimately you have to live for your own self. Allot time for silent meditation, for your soul needs meditation. Have you ever wondered what is the noblest thing on the earth? Let me answer, in the words of my Gurudev, "The noblest work is to cultivate the soul." To cultivate the soul we should sow the seeds of love, selfless service and devotion. We should chant the Name Divine, set apart time for silent communion with God, and offer the service of love to those who are less fortunate than we are. We will then experience divinity in our everyday life.

Sri Ramakrishna Paramahansa often gave the example of a goldsmith. A goldsmith burnishes the gold in the fire, he bellows the air and moulds the gold into a beautiful shape. This is a tremendous effort, after which he relaxes with his *hookah*, inhaling the aroma of tobacco. Like the goldsmith, we too should put in our best efforts and then relax in silence, inhaling and exhaling the Name Divine. The Name Divine can be of Rama, Krishna, Shiva, Jesus, Buddha or anyone who to us is symbolic of Truth.

Keep your heart pure, the heart is the seat of the Lord. Decorate the interiors of your heart with love, longing and *bhakti*. Let your heart be pure and Divine. This will happen only when you sublimate your senses, creating a pure and a loving place for the Lord to reside. Once the senses are sublimated, the Divine Energy, the positive life force will flow in. This Divine Energy is there within each one of us, but it is barricaded, blocked, suppressed by the lower emotions. Hence, we are unable to feel, to experience the beauty of the Divine Energy. We are trapped inside the darkness of the 'throat *chakra*' or *Ajna chakra*. It is the sixth *chakra* from the base, and a hindrance for the life force '*mooldhara*' pure energy to rise to *Sahasrar chakra*. Take the first step on this inner journey, discover your 'self', and the miraculous wonders of the interior world. Experience the bliss that is there within you, and belongs to you as your birthright. This journey will ultimately lead you out of the cycle of birth and death.

The 'F' of Forgiveness is freedom.
Forgiveness sets us free from
the hurts which otherwise would
continue to prick us for as long as
memory lasts.

12

Forgive and Be Free

The 16th chapter of Srimad Bhagavad Gita describes two types of attitudes – the Divine and the Demonic.

It is a common observation that in the same family every member has different behavioural traits. Some are blessed with qualities of gentleness and sweetness; and others with what is described (sometimes affectionately, sometimes accusingly) as a devilish personality – that is, they have demonic traits. They are envious, revengeful and always carry a grudge within. They may even be aggressive and cruel. We often wonder how siblings born of the same parents turn out to be so drastically different. It is true that we are born according to our *karma*. We carry the *karmic* residue of our desires, our attitudes as well as the benefits of our good actions from our previous births.

"No effort of yours is wasted," the Lord assures Arjuna. "Every good action reaps its reward; hence do not despair." The Divinity in a person is seen in his or her actions of kindness, forgiveness, love and compassion. The demonic element expresses itself in actions of revenge, envy, jealousy, the burning fire of anger, cruelty and harsh criticism of others. There are parents who are cruel to their children and even abuse them. Every other day, we hear of children who leave home, or are even driven to suicide by parental abuse and cruelty. Such parents are like tyrants; and we are left to wonder how parents could behave so cruelly towards their own children or even drive them to suicide? They are undoubtedly 'reaping' the seeds sown by their own previous *karmas*. Such people are at the bottom rung of human evolution. They carry forward the residue of the *'samskaras'* of their previous births as well as the *karmic* reactions of their own doings, in the present birth.

> Mutual forgiveness of each vice
> Such are the gates of Paradise.

It was William Blake, the great English Poet of the 18th century, who gave us these beautiful lines. He was a man with qualities of Divinity. He once said, "Divine people and those who are in Heaven, forgive others irrespective of their evil deeds. Their kindness is Universal." Forgiveness is a beautiful quality. It relieves your mind of the burden of reacting negatively to other people's actions, grudges and misconduct towards you. You can release that tension through the Divine quality of forgiveness. Forgiveness will create a tranquil space within your mind, allowing the spirit to grow in that beautiful feeling of lightness. Forgiveness makes you kind. It gives you an inner beauty. It makes you glow without and illumines you within; it transforms all those who are touched by it.

Gurudev Sadhu Vaswani, narrated to us a beautiful story of Hussain, the martyr of *Karbala*. Once he was sitting at his dinner, and the slave was present to serve him. By an accident a hot dish fell on Hussain's knees.

The slave was terrified and recited a verse from the Holy *Qur'an*, "Paradise belongs to him who restrains his anger."

Hussain answered, "I am not angry."

The slave continued, "Paradise belongs to him who forgiveth his brother."

And Hussain said, "I forgive you!"

And the slave finished the verse, "For God loves the benevolent."

Immediately, Hussain responded, "I give you liberty! No longer are you my slave: and I give you four hundred pieces of silver!"

Truly, God loves men of compassion; God loves those who forgive their fellow men!

There was a time, when our families exuded the warmth of love and serenity of peace. The family members, overlooked each other's faults, gave each other understanding, love and tolerance; they forgave each other's mistakes, supported one another in times of crisis, consoled each other in times of grief and tragedy. The families bonded in harmony, vibrating serenity and happiness. The elders were men and women of Divine qualities. Whenever the youngsters went wayward or wrong, the elders tenderly enfolded them in their love and kindness, and brought them on to the right track.

Many of the early communities were governed by their own set of rules and laws. One of the rules was 'life for life'. If someone killed a person, the victim's family, could take the law into their own hands, and take away the life of the perpetrator of the crime. The punishment prescribed was 'Death for Death'.

Let me share with you a true story of one such community. There were two friends. They were very close to each other. As often happens, the two spent most of the time together. One day, during a quarrel, things turned ugly and the situation got out of hand. One of the friends killed the other in an uncontrollable fit of rage. According to the law of the community, the family of the victim had the right to punish the killer of their son, with death penalty. They dragged the friend to their house and locked him up in a room. The family then assembled in the next room to decide on the punishment to be meted out to him. Every member of the family wanted to exercise the law, 'death for death'. They wanted to kill their son's friend. Life for life, death for death: they echoed unanimously. It was the grandfather of the murdered boy, who raised his voice and silenced everyone. He said, "No! Our dear boy is already dead. We are in grief. We know the sorrow of such a terrible loss. By killing the criminal, we will gain nothing. On the other hand, his family will lose him and go through the same grief and pain that we feel now. They will endure the same suffering, pain and agony as we are going through. What can we possibly gain by inflicting such meaningless suffering on them?"

For quite sometime the family debated on the matter. The boy who was locked up in the room feared the worst. He thought, "My time is up. I am finished." He regretted his criminal act. He had brutally killed his friend whom he loved so dearly. What kind of devil had possessed him and led him to such an act? At the same time, the family after much rumination and deliberation, decided to spare the boy and forgive him. Imagine the boy's surprise, when he was released and allowed to leave the house in which he had been held captive!

Ali-Ibn-Al-Husain was a man of God, and the son-in-law of Prophet Muhammad. Once a man came to him and said, "I met a man who abused and cursed you." Husain said, "Take me to him." So the conveyor of the bad news took him to the attacker thinking that Ali-Ibn-Al-Husain would fight with him and inflict revenge upon him. But, when they met the concerned man, Husain only said to him, "If what you say is true, may God forgive me; and if what you say is not true may God Almighty forgive you."

True forgiveness does not contribute to egoism and vanity. There is a beautiful saying about the violet, which spreads fragrance on the hand that crushes it. We too, must forgive silently, unostentatiously.

There was a poor elderly maid servant, whose task it was to make the royal beds on which the King and Queen slept.

On a beautiful, full-moon night, the King and Queen decided that they would sleep on the terrace of the Royal Palace, open to the sky. The old maid worked hard to lay the huge royal mattresses with their expensive and elaborate sheets and pillows. By the time the laborious task was finished, she was so exhausted that she sat down for a while to rest. The gentle breeze and the coolness of the moonlit night lulled her to sleep. Unaware of what she was doing, she lay on the royal bed and fell asleep.

You can imagine the wrath and ire of the Royal couple when they discovered the humble, shabby figure of the old servant on their beautiful bed! The Queen was beside herself with rage and ordered the royal attendant to lash her fifty times with a whip.

Trembling and humiliated, the servant bowed down low and felt the first furious whiplash on her back. She cried out in great agony. The second blow descended, and she screamed, yet again.

The third and the fourth followed in quick succession. She was silent. The sixth, seventh, eighth blow fell – without even a movement from her. After the tenth, she started to laugh out aloud!

The attendant could not continue whipping any longer. He was stunned and amazed! How could she laugh in the face of such searing pain and humiliation?

The King and Queen were also nonplussed by her behaviour. "Why are you laughing?" they demanded of her.

"You were not ready to forgive me my single offence," said the maid. "But, I learnt to forgive you after the pain of the first two blows. But this thought amuses me, that for the pleasure of lying ten minutes upon a velvet mattress, I am condemned to be whipped fifty times. I thought of the fate of monarchs like you, who sleep on such beds every night of your life – I wondered how many lashes you would merit!"

The King realised the wisdom of her words and ordered the maid to be released immediately.

Many people ask me, "How can I forgive someone who keeps on hurting me? At one time or another, I feel like retaliating. After all, it is said that one can expect an eye for an eye…"

Mahatma Gandhi once said, "An eye for an eye would leave the whole world half-blind." Hatred begets hatred. Vengeance begets vengeance. It is only the magic of forgiveness that can break the vicious cycle. The most intense hatred and bitterness can be conquered with the all-powerful healing force of forgiveness.

Think of Guru Amardas! He succeeded Guru Angad. Guru Angad's son, Datu, was disappointed. He felt it was his right to occupy the *Guru-gadi* (the seat of the Master). Full of anger, he came to Guru Amardas and said, "Till yesterday, you were but a servant in our home. Today, you have occupied the *Guru-gadi*!" So saying, he kicked the aged Guru.

The Guru looked at him with compassionate eyes and said, "I am an old man and my bones are hard. They must have hurt your foot. Forgive me."

Such is the witness of the holy ones, the Saints of God, who have appeared in all climes and in all countries.

Think of Rishi Dayanand, the illustrious founder of the *Arya Samaj*. He was known for his fearlessness and frankness. He spoke the truth without fear or favour and, in the process, won the displeasure of many influential people. Some of them bribed his cook, Jagannath, to administer slow poison in his food.

Rishi Dayanand became seriously ill. The doctors realised that the great leader had been poisoned and there was no hope of recovery. When Rishi Dayanand learnt of it, he called Jagannath and, giving him some money, said, "Escape to Nepal. Flee, while there is time. If my disciples learn of what has happened, they will kill you!"

Every great man has borne witness to the noble ideal of forgiveness.

Once, thieves entered the *ashram* of Sri Ramana Maharishi at night. They were under the impression that they would find lots of money and expensive objects in the *ashram*, for the Maharishi had several wealthy followers and devotees who constantly visited him. But, to their anger and dismay, they found practically nothing worth stealing.

Suddenly they entered an inner chamber, where they came upon the Maharishi in deep meditation. Rudely they accosted him, demanding that he tell them where the money and valuables were kept. Getting no response from him, the men began to attack him.

A few disciples who had been awakened by the commotion rushed into the Maharishi's room, and were appalled by the sight that met their eyes. As for the thieves, they took to their heels and fled from the *ashram* in no time.

Incensed by the injury inflicted on their Beloved Guru, the disciples seized sticks and stones and whatever they could lay their hands on, and decided to pursue the miscreants.

"Do not go after them," said the Maharishi. "Pause and reflect for a minute. If your teeth bite your tongue, do you knock them off?"

The disciples learnt the profound spiritual lesson that all of us – all human beings – are linked in a cosmic chain of Being. Where then, is there room for anger and resentment when others are a part of us, and everyone is part of a great Cosmic Whole?

Guru Ramdas was out asking for his daily *biksha* (alms). He came to the door of a cottage and called, "Please give me the alms, mother!"

The woman of the house was busy mopping the floor of the hut. "Go away!" she called. "I'm busy and I have nothing to give you!"

"Please give me something – anything!" begged the Saint.

The woman came out in a rage. "You shorn-headed, useless beggar!" she shouted. "Why do you harass honest, hard-working people everyday?"

"You are right, mother," agreed the Guru, "but I beg you to give me alms."

The irate woman threw the dirty water and the mopping cloth at him and shouted, "Take that and be gone!"

"God Bless you dear Mother!" said the Saint, taking the bit of cloth. He went to the river and washed himself and went home. He had nothing to eat that day, and sat down in deep meditation.

When he came out of his *samadhi*, he realised it was evening. He prepared for the daily *aarti*, but found that there was no wick for the lamp. His eye fell on the piece of cloth that the woman had thrown at him, and he tore it up to make several wicks. When the *aarti* was over, he said to himself, "God is infinitely kind, and out of the dirty piece of cloth thrown at me, bright and lighted wicks could be made! May God bless that woman!"

Hatred and jealousy, anger and bitterness, are aroused in us due to *karmic* influences. When we allow ourselves to be overcome by such hatred, we are linking ourselves to the *karmic* processes of those whom we regard as our 'enemies'. The best way to overcome this adverse process is to return love for hatred; charity for anger; compassion for cruelty; and forgiveness for all wrongs done to us.

Attachment is the root of sorrow.
No one belongs to you: you belong
to the Lord. Therein lies the secret
of the art of living.

13

If You Would Be Happy?

Gurudev Sadhu Vaswani often narrated to us the story of a slave who was a man of true knowledge. The slave was born abroad but he had great devotion for Lord Sri Krishna. He had read and imbibed the teachings of the *Srimad Bhagavad Gita*. The slave was born 19 centuries ago. In those early days slavery was common. Slaves were bought and sold like commodities in the market. Slaves were often ill-treated, but with the passing of centuries, enlightenment dawned on society and gradually slavery was abolished. Slavery is indeed an inhuman practice.

Even today, there are many social evils which need to be eradicated. If we want our civilisation to survive the test of time, then we will have to refine our habits. It is a shame that the animal is considered as a commodity and is traded in the market, either for consumption as food or as a mode of transport. Just as slavery was abolished two centuries ago, similarly in this century the birds and animals must be saved from the torture of human beings. A day will come when meat eating will be considered as murder. When a man kills another man, he is called a murderer. But when a man kills an animal for food, he is spared all punishment. I hope and pray that a day will come when man will not kill animals for his pleasure or his food.

The slave we are referring to was bought by a man who was a hard taskmaster. The slave was made to slog throughout the day doing hard physical chores. The slave did his work silently, always accepting it as a gift from God. This slave was a true *yogi*. A true *yogi* is one who thanks God for everything that befalls him under all circumstances and all conditions. A true *yogi*, according to the *Srimad Bhagavad Gita*, is above the *dwandas* (binaries) of sorrow and joy. A true *yogi* is an evolved soul who is ever grateful to God for whatever he gets. There was something about this slave which raised curiosity in his master.

One night, his master returned late. He saw that the slave was on his knees offering prayers to God. Intrigued by what he saw, the following night, the master again observed the slave. He saw once again that the slave was totally immersed in his prayers. Touched by his devotion, the master felt a profound sense of compassion for him. He knew that the slave slogged throughout the day and yet every night he prayed to God in gratitude seeking His blessings. This gesture of the slave surprised the master. He wondered how a slave, who has nothing to show for his possessions and everything to bear by way of drudgery and hard labour, could thank God and seek His blessings. Somewhere this touched his heart and the realisation dawned on him, that he, who had so much wealth and lived in great luxury, had never thanked God nor ever prayed in devotion.

Awakened, the master goes to his slave and says, "Forgive me. For, I have sinned." The slave remained silent and did not utter a word. A true *yogi* or *bhakta* does not speak much. He bears his suffering silently.

When the master repeated his apology, the slave replied to him, "Why do you ask for forgiveness? In fact it is I who should ask you. If I have made a mistake or misbehaved in any way, then please tell me, so that I can correct myself." Hearing this, his master began to weep. For, he realised that he had sinned against nature and God's laws, by buying a human being as a slave. He repented his action; he felt that his slave was the wronged man, the victim, and yet he had uttered not a word of complaint against the inhuman treatment meted out to him.

Enlightened by the words of the slave, the master opened his heart and said to him, "From today onwards you are free. You can do whatever you like with your time." Hearing this, the slave rejoiced. For, in his heart there was a deep desire to devote more time in remembrance of God.

The very next day the slave bid farewell to his master. The maser said to him, "Listen brother, there is no need for you to go anywhere in search of food and shelter. You can continue to live in my house as you have done till now. I will feel truly blessed if you remained under my roof."

The slave agreed to stay behind and began to divide his time between the service of his master and his prayerful worship. After sometime, he decided to go out to the world, spreading the message of God. As is always the case, some people mocked at him, others heard him. He asked people, "Tell me, are you all happy?" The reply would be negative. He would then speak to them of a path that led to happiness. People were impressed by his wisdom. Gradually, people came under his influence and began to spread his message of happiness.

Soon, he set up a little *ashram* and began to give discourses on life and human nature and the secret of true happiness. His words of wisdom were eagerly absorbed by the seekers who thronged to hear him. His eager disciples compiled his teachings into a book, which remains an invaluable treasure of spiritual thoughts. It has been translated into many languages of the world. The book has the essence of *Srimad Bhagavad Gita*. One of the beautiful thoughts expressed in the book is –

"If you want to be a good human being, then you should be aware of the evil within you."

When a man falls ill he goes to the hospital to be treated. Even so, when man realises that he is full of evil, he should go to *satsang*. *Satsang* is like the hospital, which will treat the disease called 'evil'.

What is the most common disease which afflicts man? It is 'attachment'. All our attachment is with the illusions of this world. Attachment is universal and so is the sorrow or suffering that goes with it. Every human being who is attached, has to bear suffering and face trials and tribulations of life, irrespective of his wealth or social status.

What is the cause of all suffering? Why are we so unhappy?

Long ago, there was an old woman, who regularly attended our *satsang*. One day, I found her crying and weeping during the *satsang*. After the *satsang*, I went to her and asked, "What is troubling you, mother? Why are you crying?" The old woman replied, "I lost my husband many years ago. He has left behind a lot of wealth, which I have inherited. I have a young son who has fallen into bad company. He runs after girls, drinks alcohol and gambles. He is wasting his father's money in satisfying his evil desires. Every now and then he asks for money and when I refuse he beats me up. He threatens to kill me if I do not give him the money he wants."

Hearing her sorrowful tale I told her, "Mother, the solution is very easy. A police official attends our *satsang* everyday. If you permit me I will request him to deal with your son." Hearing about the policeman, the woman got frightened; she almost screamed saying, "No, No! Please do not lodge a complaint with the police against my son. He may be bad, but, he is my son."

This is attachment. Once we are trapped in this cycle of attachment our suffering begins. If this boy had been someone else's son, I am sure the old woman would have said, "Please hand him over to the police, he needs to be punished." Attachment is a malaise which has afflicted the whole world.

In this very book, the slave who was a *brahmagyani* has referred to three types of attachment. The same is also explained in the *Srimad Bhagavad Gita*. Sri Krishna speaks to Arjuna, "O Arjuna, renounce all attachment." Even Jesus Christ gave the message of non-attachment. It is difficult to practise detachment – non-attachment in our daily life.

A research scholar went to Africa to study the behaviour of monkeys. He requested his local guide to capture the monkeys, without harming them. The guide suggested various means of trapping the animal – casting a net, putting the animals to sleep with medicated darts or caging them. But, the professor and his research team wanted to study the habits of the monkeys and capturing them in the traditional way would frighten them, causing trauma and altering their behaviour. The research team discussed and debated and found an easy solution to this problem. They collected glass jars with narrow necks and filled the base with groundnuts. They placed these jars in the area frequented by the monkeys. Getting the smell of groundnuts the monkeys invaded the place. Every monkey tried to put its hand in the jar to grab the groundnuts. It was very easy for them to put their hand in the jar but it was difficult for them to bring out the hand, which was now filled with groundnuts. The monkeys were stuck with the glass jars, with one hand inside it. Naturally, the monkeys cried out for help and one by one they were all captured.

Our condition too, is very similar to the situation faced by these monkeys. We too, like the monkeys, want to grab a few peanuts and in the bargain get caught in the ropes of attachment. The rope keeps tightening because we do not let it go. Attachment binds us to the world.

There are three kinds of attachment: the first is attachment to wealth. The second attachment is to comforts and luxuries. Most of us are comfort loving. We want to enjoy everything. 'I want to enjoy my life,' is the buzzword of the youth today. The third attachment is love for name and fame. Everyone wants to be superior to others. Everyone wants to climb the social ladder, everyone wants to be at the top of their career and everyone wants to be one up on the other.

As I said earlier, attachment is a disease. What is the cure for this disease?

The only way to renounce all attachments is to imbibe the true values of life. The slave in his book writes that towns and cities are not created out of bricks, by buildings and bridges. The cities are created by true education. Open schools that impart true education. Let the students be brought up in the 'rishi culture'. True education would enlighten the students, that whatever exists is a gift from the Above. We are not the owners of whatever is bestowed upon us, we are merely the trustees. This puts a great responsibility on all of us, because as trustees, we have to discharge our duties faithfully.

The slave-philosopher also urges us not to grieve excessively over any loss. Life on this earth is meant to end in death, and none of us are exceptions to this rule. As the famous essayist Joseph Addison once remarked, we must be aware of, "the futility of mourning for those whom we must surely follow". Therefore, we must not grieve over the loss of a beloved or a dear one. For, in the first place they did not belong to us; they were just gifts from God, not to be retained but to be returned. God gives us these rare, precious dear ones, so that we may take good care of them, love them, tend to them and not try to possess their body and soul.

To sum up the teachings of this great man: Share your wealth, your time with those less fortunate than you. Everything given by God is a loan. Our very breath of life is a 'trust' which is to be spent in the service of others. May we all surrender ourselves at the Lotus Feet of the Lord and give, give and give all that we have in the service of humanity.

Service is a debt, a rent we have
to pay for inhabiting the human
body. It is a debt, a rent we have to
pay for the many favours that we
have received from God and the
surrounding Universe.

14

Three Forms of Discipline

There is a profoundly moving thought expressed in the *Guru Granth Sahib*, the holy scripture of the Sikhs: *Hukme andar sabhkoi, baher hukum na koi.*

Everything that happens, happens according to the Will of God. Not a leaf, not a blade of grass can so much as move in the breeze, without His Will. The whole, magnificent phenomenon of the universe is the expression of His Will. We live and breathe and move and act as He Wills.

This world is ephemeral; men and women come here and depart at His Will. Death is perpetually dancing at his doorstep, yet man clings to his life, to his worldly possessions, as if they belong to him for ever and ever more. But, these treasures are ours only for a brief duration; they have to be left behind. We cannot carry our worldly treasures with us to the world beyond this one. The only thing we can carry is *satya* – the treasure of truth.

We are all well-versed in the accumulation of worldly wealth; but how may we acquire this treasure of truth? This treasure of truth is a rejuvenating, revitalising energy. The treasure of truth is not the result of any worship or rituals. It is the reality of awakening the *shakti* within. The recurring question that we must ask ourselves again and again is this: how can we awaken this *shakti* within? Our sages and saints tell us that in order to awaken the *shakti* within, we have to observe certain disciplines, follow certain rules.

The first discipline is *Naam Simran* – chanting the Name Divine. Our life is a field, wherein, if we sow the positive seeds of the Name Divine, we would surely reap a rich harvest of Divinity. Therefore, let us invest our time and effort in chanting the Name Divine. Let our lives be so permeated with the fragrance of the Name Divine, that it may wipe away the evil odour of our past *karmas*. The Name Divine will plough through our evil desires, all our negative emotions of hate and greed, and leave the field of our hearts ready to receive His Divine grace. The *yuga* (era) we are passing through is a dark one indeed. Hence, chant the Name Divine and bring enlightenment into your life. The best time to chant or to recite the Name Divine is early in the dawn.

One of the most powerful phrases you can repeat is *Om Tat Sat* or *Om Shanti, Om Shanti:* recite this as a *mantra* and you will find that your mind becomes one-pointed; it will stop its futile wandering, and will gradually become integrated. When you sit in silence to meditate or to chant, do not worry about the wandering mind. It is the mind's nature to wander. Let the mind play truant, while you continue with your chant.

The second discipline is Service. The best service that human beings can aspire to is the service of saints and sages. By serving the saints, we are blessed with a fraction of their vibrant power, and some of their positive spiritual energy. Being in the vicinity of a saint and serving him with devotion is very beneficial to our spiritual progress, for it bestows the grace of the Lord on us. If you are not able to serve a saint or a holy one personally, then serve the poor and the broken ones, for they too are images of God. Learn to share your money and wealth with those who are less fortunate than you.

Gurudev Sadhu Vaswani used to tell us, "I have but one tongue, but if I had a thousand tongues, with each one of them I would still utter the one word, 'Give, Give, Give'."

Give without any expectation of reward. Do not condescend towards the receivers; do not patronise them; do not imagine that you are doing someone a favour by giving something to them. Rather, thank God for giving you the opportunity to serve others. When you give, you are not obliging others. On the contrary, you must feel obligated to God, for having given you this wonderful opportunity of serving others.

In the age old traditions of Indian culture, the daughter-in-law of the house is expected to be reverent to her in-laws and obey them. In one such household of a rich businessman, the daughter-in-law was dismayed and disappointed by her father-in-law's 'show' of outward behaviour. The businessman had put on the mask of a philanthropist, but in reality, he was a mean and miserly man. He would distribute all the useless, unwanted things of the household, rotten grains and poor quality food among the poor and the needy, in the name of social service and charity. The daughter-in-law was a woman of values. She prayed to God to give her an opportunity to set her father-in-law on the right path. One day, her mother-in-law travelled out of the city and she had the opportunity to serve meals to her father-in-law. The daughter-in-law made *chappatis* (Indian Bread) from inferior quality wheat, the same wheat which was to be distributed to the poor people that day, in another show of charity. Naturally the *chappatis* turned out hard and dark brown. When the businessman was served his food, he noticed that the *chappatis* were not of the usual quality that he had everyday. He wondered why his daughter-in-law had served him such poor quality *chappatis*. Angry and puzzled, he called his daughter-in-law and began to grill her.

"Do you know who am I? I am the head of the family," he said.

"Yes, I am aware of that," replied the daughter-in-law.

"Then why have you served me these rotten *chappatis?*" he asked. "I am a wealthy man. I can afford the best of food. Why do you feed me as if I were a beggar?"

The daughter-in-law replied, "Dear father-in-law, whatever you give to others, comes back to you some day. It is better that you get habituated to eating these *chappatis,* for they are what you are giving away to others. Sooner or later, they will come back to you as your *karma.*"

The businessman was startled; he did not like what he heard, but he soon realised the truth of her words. We all know the familiar saying, "As you sow, so shall you reap." Therefore, let us give the best, when we are giving to others. What we give to others, invariably comes back to us.

The third *sadhana* or spiritual discipline is *Bhakti.* What is *Bhakti? Bhakti* is deep love and adoration for the Creator of this Universe. This kind of love does not come suddenly. It is cultivated through *Naam Simran,* through service to others and by being kind to one and all.

When man begins to understand the reality of his existence, and the reality of the Universe, he is mystified. He is in awe of the Supreme Creator and he begins to love Him. Love creates yearning and the yearning becomes a flame. Once the flame is lit it grows into a sacred fire which destroys all that is evil and negative in our body and mind.

This love, this yearning, this pining and this pain of separation from the Beloved is a blessing which comes through the grace of the Guru. Life without this ache for the Beloved, without yearning for Him is indeed futile.

The world glitters with so many pleasures, with so many temptations of the senses that constantly lure us away from the reality of life; but man should turn a blind eye to all the glittering *maya,* for everything here is an illusion.

Three women who had been friends since childhood, met one another after a long interval. Naturally, the talk soon turned to their married life. The first one said, "My husband is indifferent to all concerns about me or the family. In fact he has shut out the world."

Her friend asked, "What do you mean?"

The woman replied, "Everyday after his bath, he sits down on his chair to pray. I keep the chair ready for him to pray near the window. One day, I forgot to put the chair in its usual place. Do you know what my dear husband did? Not realising that there was no chair, he sat on the window sill to pray. In the course of his chanting, he actually fell down. He did not even realise that he had fallen down, so engrossed was he in his prayers."

Hearing this, the second friend said, "I tell you, my husband is even worse than yours. He gets so absorbed in his *bhakti,* that when he sees that his plate is empty on the dining table, he thinks that he has finished his meals and gets up without eating anything."

The third friend said, "My husband is even more absent minded. One day, he met me in the vegetable market, where I had gone to buy vegetables. He looked at me and said, 'I have seen you somewhere, but am not able to place you'!"

You do not have to be absent minded and unaware like these three men. In fact you should always be aware and alert and awakened from within. The awareness which comes from deep within is a throbbing pain, but the same aching pain gradually subsides and eventually turns into peaceful bliss! A stage will come when you would hunger for this kind of an ache, which will draw you close to your Beloved.

There are many paths which will lead you to your goal. Counting rosary beads, worshipping the Lord at temples, going on pilgrimages and taking dips in holy rivers are all good; but the easiest path is the *sahaj marg,* the easy, natural, simple path that takes you within is through *bhakti.* May the Almighty God evoke deep yearning within you. May you realise the true treasures of New Life – those treasures which you can carry with you on your onward journey to the world beyond.

You cannot change things by
worrying over them. However, you
will find miraculous things happen if
only you believe.

15

Miracles Still Do Happen

A great philosopher of the ancient world: Epictetus once said, "There is only one way to happiness and that is to cease worrying about things which are beyond the power of our will."

I can hear many of you murmuring, "Cease worrying! Easier said than done!"

It is in the nature of the mind to worry. I doubt whether any of us ever go to bed without having worried about something or the other during the day. But many of us worry about imaginary problems. I feel the mind has two enemies which can undermine our functioning: one is worry and the other is fear. The two together, I think, can actually destroy a human being. Samuel Ullman says, "Years may wrinkle the skin, but to give up enthusiasm, wrinkles the soul. Worry, fear, self-distrust bows the heart and turns the Spirit back to dust."

A woman came to me sometime ago. She had a problem. She was blessed with everything an ordinary human being could possibly desire: but she simply could not bring herself to sit in silence and meditate. She had a good home and a family, a loving and caring husband, and obedient children who respected her every wish. How many women are so fortunate? Yet, her main problem was worry. Whenever she found time, (which was quite often), she would sit down to meditate. But the moment she sat down, all kinds of worries would begin to gnaw at her mind. She said to me, "I try to use my reason and comfort myself. Yet, my mind does not stop worrying. What should I do?"

I said to her, "The best antidote to worry is faith. To dispel your worry, all you need to do is chant the Name Divine. Just sing, *Re Mann Tu Kyun Chinta Kare? Dhyan Hari Ka Kyun Na Dhare!* – Why do you worry? Just chant the Name Divine."

It is easy to ask that question, but difficult to find the answer! But, left to itself, untrained, undisciplined and uncontrolled, it is the nature of the mind to churn out worries and brew fear. Worry is the malignancy which eats away the insides of a man. What is the cure for worrying? The cure for worrying is faith. Where there is faith, there can be no worry, because faith is an illumination: faith is light. Worry, on the other hand, is darkness. Where there is light there cannot be darkness. Therefore, we must learn to dispel all worries with the Light of faith.

A famous man once observed: "I believe God is managing affairs and that He doesn't need any advice from me. With God in charge, I believe everything will work out for the best in the end. So what is there to worry about?" Can you guess who said these apt words? Not a priest, not a renunciate, but a hard headed industrialist, and one of the outstanding enterpreneurs of his time, Henry Ford!

I sometimes find myself reflecting: "O man, the energy you waste in worrying, if converted into chanting of Name Divine, it would help you in leading a blessed and a balanced life! But let me add, chanting should not be superficial; it should not be done by merely mouthing the words or by counting the beads of a rosary. True chanting comes from within. It comes from the depths of the heart. Only then does the mind become still and devoid of worry."

God needs a heart full of love. At times, I wonder what would be God's reaction to the numerous chantings done so mechanically in the temples and on the banks of the rivers; to the worship of deities and spirits, to the rituals which are performed as mere rites! Rituals are meaningless when performed without the emotion of love. God does not count the beads of the rosary; but He does hear the sighs of longing and love that we offer to Him.

There was a humble labourer. Every evening after his work, he would go to a temple to join in the evening worship. One day, due to an emergency in his factory, he could not reach the temple on time. All the while that he was away from the evening worship, he felt restless, because his thoughts were on the *pooja* and the *aarti* that would be going on at the temple. After his duty, he rushed to the temple for worship. Out of breath, panting heavily, he entered the temple and found that the *pooja* was over and the priest was leaving the temple. With a heavy heart, the labourer asked, "Is the worship over?" The priest replied, "Yes, the worship got over just now." Hearing this, the labourer rent out a heart wrenching sigh. It was as if he had lost the most precious thing of his life. Hearing this, the priest said to him, "I am willing to exchange the fruit of my worship of so many years, for that sigh of longing!" The labourer replied, "I am willing to do so." That night, the labourer had a dream, in which he saw Sri Krishna, who said to him, "You have struck a bad bargain." The labourer was surprised. He asked, "How?" Krishna replied, "That one soulful sigh was invaluable in My estimation. It was worth much more than thousands of *poojas* offered at the temple." God needs this kind of love.

Worship, reading of the scriptures, blowing conch shells are all external rituals. But, what God wants from us is devotion which comes from the heart. A pure heart when filled with love expresses itself in a stream of tears. Our hearts are not pure. They are easily stained by the allurements and entanglements of the world.

One way to keep away from the allurements of the world is to attend *satsang* regularly. *Satsang* is a place of hope and serenity; it is a place of positive vibrations which protect us from the negativity of the world. The temptations of the world are many and its allurements are powerful. They can easily drag us into the whirlwind of worry.

One day, a seeker on the path, knocked at the door of a Guru. A voice from inside the room asked, "Who is there?" The devotee replied, "It is me." The voice from inside said, there is no place for two me's here. There is only one Being here, the Supreme Being. You may please go back."

After many years, the devotee returned and knocked once again. The voice from inside asked, "Who is there?" He replied, "My Beloved, there is only One and that is You." At once the door opened, the Guru himself came out and embraced the seeker. The Guru said, "We are One. There is neither me nor I. We have always been One." This is the Principle of Oneness.

As we are the children of God, we are a part of Him, we are a speck, a ray of the Supreme Being. How can we be separate from Him? There is Oneness all around us. We have to realise and experience this Oneness. With this experience the Light of faith will shine, dispelling the darkness of worry. God is our Father, it is His promise to each one of us, to protect us, to guard us and to guide us to safety. All that He wants in return is that we must be aware of His Being and His presence amongst us at every moment of our life.

Man worries because he holds himself responsible for everything. Once he puts his faith in God, he will realise that his responsibilities are God's responsibilities: and He will surely shoulder them according to His Will and in the perfect manner, because He Himself is the Ultimate Perfection.

Once, a holy man was sitting under the shade of a tree. He saw a line of ants, each carrying a grain of sugar. The holy man told his disciples, "See, how God takes care of ants. He will surely take care of you too. Do not worry, only remember Him." A young man, who was sitting by him and was a university graduate, blurted out, *"Swamiji,* it is true that God takes care of ants. But their needs are limited. Man needs everything. Man is different from ants, you cannot compare the two." At that moment birds were flying in the sky. The holy man pointing to them said, "Behold, God takes care of the birds flying in the sky. Why will He not take care of you?" The man was not convinced and he argued, "Birds have wings. They can fly, they can go and pick up their grains. But man cannot do so." Around the same time, an elephant happened to pass by. The holy man said, "Look at this elephant. God sees to it that he gets his food. O man, why will He not take care of you? He will surely take care of you, only you should have faith in Him."

A legend tells us that once God was asked, "The Creation of the Universe is complete. Now what is your next project?" God replied, "All My energies are now focussed on My devotees, especially those who have reposed all their faith in Me. To them, God is there to take care of all their needs. They do not care about anything. For them, I am there to take care of all their needs. They have given Me their power of attorney. Their responsibility is My responsibility. I am all the time busy taking care of them."

Shah Abdul Latif was a *sufi* saint, of the first order. Once, people asked him to ride a wild horse. The horse would not allow anyone to mount upon it, leave alone ride it. Shah Abdul Latif mounted the horse without any fuss and taking the bridle in his hand said, "God, the bridle is in Your Hand. I have no fear."

When man has cent percent faith in God, miracles happen. God takes care of everything.

Sind is famous for its spirituality. Sind is a land of *pirs* and *fakirs*. One of the most famous *fakirs* was Vatayun. Vatayun *fakir* was a mystic and a mendicant. He always said, "God Himself provides everything for me." But a day came in his life when he had to go without food. "One day is not enough to test God. Let me wait for some more time," he thought. Next day, a crowd of people were having a picnic on the river bank. They had brought utensils and cooked food by the side of the river. The food spread a rich aroma of flavours. After the food was cooked, it was suggested that a plate full of food should be dedicated to the Lord. The picnickers looked around for a suitable person who could be given the plate of savouries. They noticed Vatayun *fakir* and called him and offered him the plate of food. After eating his food Vatayun *fakir* returned home. People asked him, "Where did you disappear yesterday?" He replied, "Yesterday, I went to test God. I wanted to confirm the truth that God really takes care of our needs." People asked him, "What did you find?" Vatayun *fakir* replied, "Yes, it is true that God does provide for each one of us. But He asks for patience."

God will do everything for us, provided we have faith in Him. We have to have faith in Him and also patience. We should pray and wait for the faith to work.

Christopher Columbus, was a famous adventurous traveller. He worked to discover a new sea route to India. He embarked on his perilous journey on a ship along with the crew members. Even after sailing for months on the sea, they could not see any signs of land. They had exhausted all the stores of food and water on the ship. Yet, no shore was in sight. The crew members were frustrated. They schemed to throw Columbus into the sea. When Columbus came to know of this, he pleaded to them to give him another 48 hours. For 48 hours, Columbus prayed seeking help from God.

When everything fails, is not God our final refuge? He rescues us from despair and finds a way out.

Columbus too had reached the end of his tether. He could see only water around him and no land in sight. He prayed to God, "O God, please help me. Let me sight land." Before the deadline was over, Columbus was able to sight land. The land they had sighted was not India but a part of the Great American Continent. Christopher Columbus thus discovered America.

I would like to share with you a true story of faith and prayer. There lived a happily married couple by the name of John and Ann in the City of New York. John was a good natured, helpful man. He was loved by all. The year 1968 was an eventful one for the couple. In March that year, as John was coming down the stairs, he fell down and was hurt in the head and stomach. The doctor treated him and he was allowed to go home. A few days later, as he was driving, he seemed to go blank, and his car went out of control, dashing against an electric pole. He was again hurt in the head. A few days later, he was taking a walk, when his foot slipped and he was hurt in the head for the third time. Unfortunately, neither he nor the doctors took these injuries seriously. Each time, he received treatment as an out patient and was allowed to return home with a bandage or a few stitches.

A few days later, in the month of April, John had to receive a few of his relatives at the airport. He requested his close friend to lend him a station wagon so that he could receive his relatives from the airport. His friend willingly obliged him and John brought his relatives home. Thereafter, he went to return the station wagon to his friend. The friend who was kind and generous volunteered to drop him back. But John insisted on walking back home.

Back home, John's wife waited anxiously for his return. When it was past midnight she called up John's friend and enquired about her husband. She was told that he had left long back, as he preferred walking back home rather than being dropped by his friend. Hearing this, Ann became panicky. She reported the matter to the police. She went personally to search for him in hospitals and in other places but, she could not even find a clue to his mysterious disappearance. She prayed to God to protect John, her dear husband. She prayed that he may be safe and sound wherever he was. She prayed day and night, as she loved John.

Years passed by, and friends and family members urged Ann to re-marry. But Ann remained firm in her faith that one day, God would send her John back to her. She believed in God, and her fidelity to her husband remained unshaken. She was sure that John was alive and they would be united once again.

On the other hand, John, as he was walking back home on that fateful night, was struck by severe migraine. Unable to bear the pain, he fell down unconscious. When he awoke, he went blank. He had lost his memory and could not understand where he was and what he was doing. He boarded a train and got down at a railway station. He was so disoriented that he boarded several trains and finally arrived at a strange place. He went out in search of some work and when he was asked for his name, he became blank again. He looked at a hoarding across the road and read the words, 'James Peter'. So wherever he went, he called himself James Peter. He found a good job. Fifteen years passed by, and he still did not recollect his past.

It was December 1983. Ann still hoped that someday her John would return to her. For fifteen years Ann had not celebrated Christmas, but now with firm faith in God and a prayer in her heart, she decided to celebrate Christmas as usual. She hoped that her John would come and be united with her on the holy Christmas day. Early that December, John had another fall and was injured in the head. 'James Peter' now made an exit, and John returned. Now John could recollect his past, his memory had revived. He remembered that he lived in New York and had a wife by the name Ann. He recollected the place where he lived and his home. He began to tremble, his heart beat faster. He took a train to New York City right away, recognising and remembering all the old familiar haunts. Without any trouble, he found his way back to his home, although he was unsure of what was in store for him. He climbed up the familiar staircase and knocked on the door of his house. At that time Ann was on her knees praying.

She opened the door and both were astonished to see each other. They could not believe that this was true—was it a reality or a dream? Both rubbed their eyes and blinked at each other. Was this 1968 or 1983? Was this true? Then lovingly, they embraced each other, and wept their hearts out. It was indeed a miracle.

Ann narrated to John the saga of her faith. How for fifteen long years she had waited for him with hope and a prayer in her heart. Ann told her husband that it was her faith that had kept her alive. It was her faith too, which had kept her love and his memory alive. She told John that nothing had changed since he had left, and she had only waited and waited for his return.

This true story teaches us that we must face life's challenges and troubles with patience and faith in God. When our faith in God is absolute, He will take care of us.